THE NEGOTIATION NINJA

HOW TO MASTER THE MOST IMPORTANT SKILL IN BUSINESS

DONOVAN GARETT

AlgoRhythms Studios, Ltd.

P.O. BOX 35643

Cleveland, Ohio 44135, U.S.A

DISCLAIMER. This publication is intended (but not guaranteed) to provide accurate information in regard to the subject matter covered. Some information may not be applicable to every reader or every situation. It is sold with the understanding that neither the author, publisher nor any other person or entity connected with the creation, publication or distribution of this publication provides legal, accounting, real estate or other professional services. If expert assistance is required, the services of a competent professional should be sought. Furthermore, this publication may contain business strategies, marketing methods, and other statements that, regardless of the experiences of some, may not produce the same results for you.

PRINT ISBN: 978-1-963267-11-2

E-BOOK ISBN: 978-1-963267-12-9

AUDIOBOOK ISBN: 978-1-963267-13-6

Library of Congress Control Number: 2024915043

Printed in the United States of America

To Shar

1979 – 2024

"The key is in not spending time, but in investing it"

— Stephen R. Covey

Contents

Preface

We assume we have certain skills when starting our careers or businesses. But just as often, we find that the skills we thought we possessed are either not truly there or not refined enough to get us where we need to be.

Among the most underemphasized skills in life is the art of skillful negotiation. We have been conditioned to accept the lie that if you work hard, life will give you what you deserve.

Nothing could be further from the truth.

After decades of not getting what I wanted from people who were not interested in my long-term well-being, I can speak to this firsthand. Throughout my career, I've agonized over raises that never came, withheld promotions, and earned far less than my worth.

I have learned one simple but profound truth:

"We never get what we deserve in life.
We get what we successfully negotiate for."

After many years, I decided to write this book because I want you to get far more out of life than your past self has allowed.

This book is dedicated to helping you achieve just that.

— Donovan Garett

Introduction

Have you ever walked away from a deal and thought, *"That's it?!?!"*

That sinking feeling, the knot in your stomach, and the swirl of doubts racing through your mind can feel overwhelming.

It's a moment all too familiar to us as small business owners. You work tirelessly to set up a deal with a partner, supplier, or vendor, only to find yourself getting much less than you had originally hoped for — either sacrificing too much or not getting enough in return. Then, after the deal is done, you sit there, wondering how you ended up in this position — questioning why your negotiation skills failed you when you needed them most.

You are not alone.

Negotiation is one of the most critical, challenging, and yet underrated aspects of running a successful business (and, arguably, navigating life). It's not about winning arguments or getting your way; it's about understanding the other party's needs and finding common ground whenever possible without compromising what you value most. But when the outcome of a negotiation falls short of what you hoped it would be, it can leave you feeling defeated and unsure of your next steps.

My friend, I've been there too.

I've faced my fair share of tough negotiations. More often than I'd like to admit, I've walked away feeling like I missed out on better opportunities. I've experienced its impact on my financial stability, professional relationships, and personal well-being firsthand. The good news is that negotiating effectively is a skill that can be learned and refined.

This book is designed to guide you through the art and science of strategic negotiation. It's about empowering you with the tools and confidence you need to turn those *"That's it?!"* moments into *"That's more like it..."* outcomes. Together, we'll explore practical strategies, actionable insights, and the psychological aspects of negotiation to help you navigate even the most challenging situations.

The Way of the Ninja

Hollywood has long been fascinated by the concept of the mysterious and elusive ninja. The ability to go anywhere virtually undetected as a cunning, ruthless assassin has captured the imagination of mainstream American pop culture for decades.

However, we sometimes fail to realize that the real work of a ninja is not the mission — it's the relentless focus, preparation, and practice that occurs long before the mission even begins.

You are a negotiation ninja. You just don't realize it yet.

In the following chapters, we'll dive into the ins and outs of negotiating even the toughest terms so that you never walk away from the table with less than you deserve. Just like a ninja, the real work is about to begin — with practice, skillful reflection, and iterative improvements, your negotiating skills will be honed. With the right approach and mindset, you can master the art of negotiation and walk away from every deal feeling confident and satisfied.

Welcome to your new negotiation journey.

Welcome to the way of the ninja.

Ready? . . .

Great.

Let's begin.

CHAPTER 1
Set Clear Objectives

"Setting goals is the first step in turning the invisible into the visible."

—Anthony Robbins

What do pilots, surgeons, generals (and, yes, even ninjas) have in common?

They all follow carefully detailed plans and have clear objectives for success.

Why? . . .

Well, think about it.

Imagine a pilot slowly ascending to 30,000 feet without a flight plan, saying, *"We'll figure it out as we go along . . ."* Or, imagine being wheeled into an operating room, and the last thing you hear the surgeon say is, *"I didn't prepare a surgical plan, but we'll just wing it and hope for the best . . .*" Or, imagine a 4-Star General haphazardly gathering and leading troops into war without a carefully rehearsed battle plan.

Seems absurd, doesn't it?

These professionals operate in high-stakes environments where the cost of failure is immense. Their success depends on having clear, specific objectives that guide their decisions and actions at every step of the mission. Not having objectives is an invitation for catastrophe.

Similarly, in negotiations, having well-defined objectives allows you to steer the conversation and adapt to new information or tactics presented by the other party.

Clear goals provide direction, focus, and a benchmark for success. They enable you to confidently navigate the negotiation process, make strategic decisions, and ultimately achieve your desired results. Just as a pilot, surgeon, or general would never embark on a mission without a plan, neither should you as a negotiator.

What Are You Trying to Accomplish?

It seems like a straightforward question, but you'd be surprised how often business professionals can't articulate a clear answer.

Let me illustrate . . .

Many years ago, as a software developer, I would encounter problems that seemed to defy logic. After struggling with the problem for what seemed like an eternity, I would ask a more experienced developer, and each time I did, they would invariably start by asking me the same question:

"What, exactly, are you trying to accomplish?"

This powerful question forced me to stop and distill the complex problem swirling around in my head into a single clear goal. Once we both understood the ultimate goal, working on a path to a solution became much easier.

Similarly, when negotiating, it is critical to know your ultimate goal—or, to put it another way, *"What are you trying to accomplish?"* To do this, you need to distinguish needs vs. wants, prioritize your objectives, balance short-term and long-term goals, and make sure these goals align with your overall business strategy while also considering the other party's needs.

Identify Needs vs. Wants

Setting clear objectives begins with identifying your needs and wants. This involves distinguishing between essential and non-essential goals to ensure you focus on the most important outcomes of the negotiation. Essential goals are crucial to your success, including non-negotiable terms vital to your strategic direction.

While desirable, non-essential goals are flexible and can be adjusted or compromised to achieve mutually beneficial results. To effectively differentiate between the two, assess the impact on your business operations, profitability, and overall objectives to understand the implications of achieving or not achieving each goal.

Prioritize Your Objectives

After distinguishing between essential and non-essential goals, prioritize your objectives to focus your efforts and resources effectively.

Create a priority list by ranking your goals in order of importance, starting with those that have the greatest effect on your business. Evaluate each goal based on how well it aligns with your business strategy.

Be prepared to make concessions on lower-priority goals if necessary and maintain flexibility in your approach. If confidentiality rules allow, clearly state your top priorities during negotiations and back them up with data and evidence.

Balance Short and Long-term Goals

Balancing short-term and long-term goals is also essential for sustained success in negotiations. Short-term goals address immediate needs, delivering quick wins that support day-to-day business functions. In contrast, long-term goals focus on future growth and stability, strategic initiatives, market expansion, innovation, and building lasting partnerships. To balance them, you must ensure that immediate actions support long-term objectives.

Carefully assess your resources to set realistic and achievable objectives. Define your goals using the SMART criteria (i.e., Specific, Measurable, Achievable, Relevant, and Time-bound). Break down larger goals into smaller, manageable steps, and monitor progress regularly. Adapt your goals in response to changing circumstances and communicate them clearly to your stakeholders.

Align Objectives with Business Strategy

Aligning your negotiation objectives with your overall business strategy ensures that every negotiation supports your long-term vision, maximizing the impact of your negotiations on your business's success. Match your objectives with broader company goals such as growth targets, market expansion, innovation, and customer satisfaction to drive progress towards achieving these overarching goals.

Also, consider the impact of your negotiation objectives on your total resources, including budget, personnel, and time, to ensure efficiency. By aligning your negotiation objectives with your overall business strategy, you create a cohesive and aligned approach to negotiating.

Understand the Other Party

After clearly articulating your own needs and wants, it is vital to do the same for the other party.

Why?

Well, by accurately assessing their needs, constraints, priorities, and motivations, you can craft offers that meet their needs while simultaneously advancing your own interests. This allows you to find common ground and anticipate their moves throughout the negotiating process.

Finding areas of mutual concern is essential for creating win-win solutions in negotiations. By focusing on shared goals and identifying areas where your interests match the other party, you can enhance the likelihood of reaching a favorable agreement.

To do this, look for objectives that you both have in common. Identify areas where you both can benefit from the same result, such as negotiating a bulk order at a discounted rate. It's also important to *"play the long game,"* recognizing the value of building a long-term relationship, which often yields greater stability, trust, and opportunities for future growth.

Have a Clear Negotiation Strategy

A well-defined negotiation strategy is essential to the negotiation process. This involves creating a structured plan that combines your research and objectives, making sure you are prepared and focused throughout the negotiation.

To create a structured negotiation plan, start by clearly defining your primary and secondary objectives. Conduct background research on the other party, market conditions, and industry trends. Based on your research, develop key points and arguments, preparing data and evidence to back up your position.

It is also helpful to anticipate potential counterarguments from the other party and prepare well-reasoned responses. Plan concessions by identifying areas where you can compromise without sacrificing your core objectives. Align your research with these objectives by using credible data to plan your strategy, ensuring every decision and argument is supported by solid evidence.

Compile your research, objectives, key points, leverage points, and anticipated counterarguments into a comprehensive strategy document to serve as a reference throughout the negotiation process. Finally, be prepared to adapt based on new information or changes in negotiation dynamics while you remain focused on your main objectives.

What to Do at the Negotiating Table

While setting clear objectives is a critical component of effective negotiation, knowing what to do at the negotiating table is equally important. This involves clearly stating your goals, avoiding misunderstandings, and balancing openness with strategic disclosure.

1. State Your Goals Clearly

Here are some ways to state your goals clearly at the negotiating table:

Be Prepared. Before entering negotiations, define your primary and secondary goals. Clearly outlining what you want to achieve helps you communicate your objectives with precision. Organize your thoughts logically, using bullet points or lists to structure your main points.

Use Active Listening. Listen actively to the other party's statements and concerns. Active listening demonstrates respect and helps you understand their perspective. This may involve summarizing their points to confirm comprehension or asking clarifying questions.

Avoid Vague Language. Use simple, straightforward language, avoiding technical jargon or complex terms that might be misunderstood. Be specific about your goals and expectations. For instance, instead of saying, *"We need a good price,"* specify, *"We need a price of $X per unit."*

Use Visual Aids. Use visual aids like charts, graphs, infographics, and slides to illustrate your points. Visual aids can clarify complex information and make your objectives more tangible.

2. Avoid Misunderstandings

When stating your goals, it is important to avoid misunderstandings.

Consider these tips:

Confirm Understanding. Paraphrase the other party's statements to confirm your understanding, ensuring both sides are on the same page. Regularly summarize points of agreement and outstanding issues to reinforce understanding and keep the discussion focused. For example, say, *"So, what I'm hearing is that you are concerned about . . . Is that correct?"*

Ask Clarifying Questions. Seek clarification whenever something is unclear to prevent assumptions and ensure all details are understood. For instance, ask, *"Can you clarify what you mean by . . . ?"*

Nonverbal Communication. Be mindful of nonverbal communication, such as body language, facial expressions, and tone of voice. Nonverbal cues convey additional meaning and help gauge the other party's reactions. Notice if the other party seems hesitant or confused, and address any concerns promptly.

Feedback and Adjustments. Regularly seek feedback to ensure your communication is effective. Be open to adjusting your approach based on the feedback received. For example, ask, *"Is there anything I can explain more clearly or in more detail?"*

Avoid Assumptions. Avoid making assumptions about the other party's understanding or intentions. Always verify information and confirm mutual understanding. Instead of assuming the other party agrees with your proposal, ask directly, *"Are we all in agreement?"*

By utilizing these techniques, you can articulate your goals clearly and avoid misunderstandings during negotiations. Effective communication ensures both parties have a shared understanding, paving the way for a successful negotiation.

3. Balance Openness and Strategic Withholding

Transparency builds trust and enables more collaborative discussions. However, balancing openness with the strategic withholding of information is crucial to protect your interests while building a foundation for agreement.

Know What to Share

Share information that is essential for facilitating common understanding, such as your main objectives, key concerns, and the rationale behind your positions, but be selective about divulging non-essential details that could weaken your bargaining strength.

Share this type of information only when it contributes to mutual understanding and progress. For instance, share relevant market comparisons to justify your pricing instead of sharing internal costs.

Withhold Information Strategically

Withhold sensitive intelligence that could be used against you, such as proprietary data and strategic plans. Keep certain leverage points or fallback positions confidential until necessary to advance the negotiation to maintain negotiating power.

Phased Disclosure

Use a phased approach to disclosing information, sharing more as trust builds and negotiations continue to move in a positive direction. This allows you to gauge the other party's intentions and adjust your level of transparency accordingly. Start with general objectives and gradually provide more detailed information as you reach preliminary agreements on key terms. Encourage reciprocal sharing of information for mutual commitment.

IMPORTANT NINJA TIP: Never seek or disclose privileged information or information obtained from former employees, competitive or trade secrets, or any other information about your competitors. Pay attention to any special instructions provided by attorneys regarding disclosure. Many trade secrets are lost innocently over drinks.

Have a Contingency Plan

As stated earlier, preparation is crucial for a successful negotiation, which includes having a contingency plan. Contingency plans reduce the risks of failed negotiations and avoid business disruptions. Knowing you have a backup plan also provides confidence during negotiations, allowing for more assertive negotiation if necessary.

To develop a contingency plan, start by identifying key risks — focusing on areas where failures could significantly impact your business. Research and identify potential alternatives for each critical term, considering different suppliers, partners, or strategies. Weigh the feasibility of each alternative, considering factors like cost, time, quality, and reliability. Then, create detailed action plans for implementing each alternative, outlining responsible parties, timelines and steps to take if the negotiation fails.

Create a BATNA

You may be asking . . . *"What the heck is a BATNA?"*

A B.A.T.N.A. (or *Best Alternative to a Negotiated Agreement*)[1] is the best outcome you can achieve if the current negotiation fails. It provides leverage and helps ensure you do not accept terms worse than your best alternative.

Using a BATNA in Negotiations

When negotiating, use your BATNA to set realistic expectations and strengthen your position. Having a strong alternative discourages the other party from pushing for unfavorable terms. Regularly compare offers with your BATNA to decide whether to continue negotiating or to walk away. Your BATNA can also be used to manage concessions, ensuring the overall deal remains advantageous.

By preparing alternatives and developing a strong BATNA, you enhance your negotiating power and avoid unfavorable agreements.

---

1. In our companion course, we will dive deep into BATNAs, including how to create one and how to use it prior to negotiation. To get notified when we launch, visit https://bit.ly/nn-course

These contingency plans allow you to navigate negotiations with confidence and strategic foresight.

Common Pitfalls to Avoid

Let's discuss a couple of common pitfalls that occur when it comes to having clear negotiating objectives: 1) not considering the other party's goals; and 2) failing to adapt and re-evaluate your objectives when needed.

Overlooking the Other Party's Goals

Ignoring the other party's goals and needs can lead to a breakdown in communication, mistrust, and, ultimately, failed negotiations. If the other party's goals are not acknowledged, it becomes challenging to find common ground, leading to erosion of trust and damaged relationships. Agreements that do not consider the other party's needs are also unbalanced and unsustainable, leading to dissatisfaction and potential renegotiation.

To make sure both sides benefit, take time to understand the other party's needs and concerns. Engage in collaborative problem-solving to develop solutions that address both parties' needs. Maintain open and transparent communication for mutual understanding. Specifically, look for areas where your goals overlap. Approach negotiations with a long-term perspective, focusing on building and maintaining strong relationships.

Failing to Adapt

Flexibility is crucial in negotiations, as failing to adapt to changing circumstances or new information hinders your ability to agree on mutually beneficial terms. Flexibility demonstrates your willingness to understand and accommodate the other party's needs, creating a foundation for a collaborative relationship.

To maintain flexibility, continuously evaluate your objectives and strategies as the negotiation progresses. Set objectives that allow for adjustments and prepare for multiple possibilities. Keep the lines of communication open with the other party to understand their changing needs and adjust your objectives if possible. Finally, focus on your core interests while being open to creative solutions that may not have been initially considered. This adaptive approach ensures you are always positioned to make the most of the negotiation process.

Key Takeaways

Clear objectives are essential for successful negotiations. They provide direction, focus, and alignment with your overall strategy, helping to prevent misunderstandings. Well-defined goals promote effective decision-making by keeping the negotiation on track and avoiding unnecessary detours. When both parties understand each other's objectives, the potential for confusion and conflict is reduced.

Entering negotiations without clear and well-defined objectives can lead to unfocused and unproductive discussions, reducing leverage and resulting in poor decisions. Without specific goals, you may spend excessive time on minor issues, neglecting critical aspects of the agreement, and may end up accepting terms that do not directly support business goals. This lack of direction can also lead to missed opportunities for value creation.

Structured goal-setting breaks down major objectives into actionable steps and generally involves regular reviews and adjustments, allowing for adaptability on both sides. This ensures that the negotiation is purposeful and aimed at achieving the best possible results.

In the next chapter, we will discuss why it's critical to know your worth before entering negotiations.

CHAPTER 2

Know Your Worth

"If you don't know your own value, somebody will tell you your value, and it'll be less than you're worth."

— Bernard Hopkins

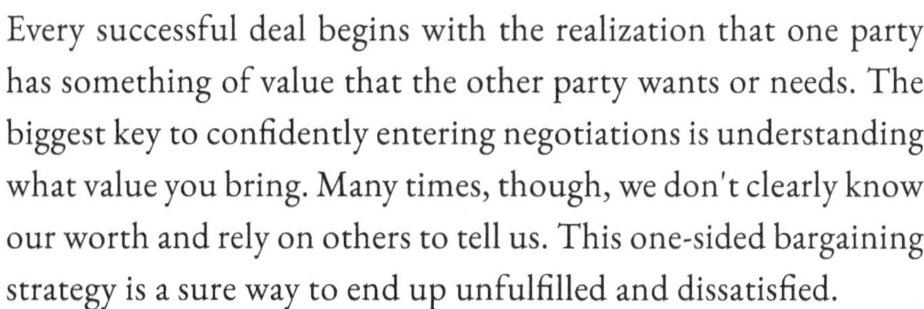

Every successful deal begins with the realization that one party has something of value that the other party wants or needs. The biggest key to confidently entering negotiations is understanding what value you bring. Many times, though, we don't clearly know our worth and rely on others to tell us. This one-sided bargaining strategy is a sure way to end up unfulfilled and dissatisfied.

Knowing your worth involves a thorough understanding of what the market will pay, analyzing credible data, considering any adjustments that are warranted given the current bargaining environment, and effectively communicating that value to the other party.

When preparing for negotiations, it's crucial to avoid both overestimating and underestimating your worth. Overestimation can lead to unrealistic expectations and demands, potentially causing negotiations to stall or fail. On the other hand, underestimating your worth can result in accepting less than you deserve or need and feeling overwhelmed, overworked, and unfulfilled. Therefore, it's essential to strike a balance by objectively knowing your worth.

Let's start with how to assess your value.

Know Your True Value

Knowing your true value involves a multi-faceted approach. It includes identifying the unique strengths your product and/or service brings to the market, evaluating the contributions that your business provides, building confidence in your negotiating position, and cultivating a positive mindset.

Let's examine these aspects together in more detail, starting with identifying your unique strengths.

Identify Your Unique Strengths

Every business has unique strengths that set it apart from the competition, including yours. These strengths form the core of your value proposition and should be clearly identified and articulated.

Consider the following aspects when identifying your unique strengths:

Product/Service Quality. Evaluate the quality of your products or services. What makes them superior to those offered by competitors?

Are there specific features, benefits, or innovations that distinguish them?

Brand Reputation. Honestly assess your brand's market reputation. A strong, well-regarded brand can be a significant asset in negotiations, as it naturally implies reliability and trustworthiness.

Customer Loyalty. Consider your customer base's loyalty. High levels of customer satisfaction and loyalty are indicators of business value and can be leveraged in negotiations.

Market Position. Analyze your position within the market. Are you a leader in your industry? Do you have a niche that you dominate? Your market position can greatly influence your negotiation power.

Evaluate Your Business's Contributions

Understanding your worth also involves evaluating your business's broader contributions to the market and the local community.

This may include:

Economic Impact. Consider your business's economic impact on the local or broader economy. Consider job creation, contributions to local development, or support for other businesses through your network/supply chain.

Innovation and Development. Reflect on the innovations and developments your business has introduced. Are you driving industry trends or leading technological advancements? Your role as an innovator can be a powerful negotiating tool.

Social and Environmental Responsibility. Assess your business's commitment to social and environmental responsibility. Increasingly, businesses are recognized and valued, not just for their financial performance but also for their contributions to social causes and the environment.

Credibility. Finally, consider the credibility or prestige that partnering with your business will provide the other party. This might include years in business, special expertise, or access to special resources, contacts, and information.

Build Your Confidence

Armed with a thorough understanding of your unique strengths, the next crucial step is to build the confidence necessary to assert your worth during the negotiation process. Having a confident approach significantly influences the final outcome of any negotiation.

Here are some practical ways to strengthen your confidence before entering negotiations:

Prepare and Practice

The basis of confidence lies in thorough preparation and practice. When you are well-prepared, you can anticipate potential challenges and respond effectively.

Consider the following strategies:

Develop a Comprehensive Plan. Create a detailed negotiation plan that outlines your objectives, key points, and potential concessions. Anticipate possible objections and prepare responses. A well-thought-out plan serves as a roadmap during negotiations, ensuring you stay focused and on track.[1]

Role-Playing and Simulation. Practice your negotiation scenarios through role-playing exercises. Ask a colleague, mentor, or friend to act as the other party. Simulate different scenarios and practice your responses. Role-playing helps you anticipate real-world challenges and refine your negotiation tactics.

Cultivate a Positive Mindset

More often than not, we are so hyper-focused on what could go wrong that we don't adequately consider what led us to the bargaining table in the first place. A positive mindset is essential for maintaining confidence during negotiations. How you perceive yourself and your abilities can significantly impact your performance.

These strategies will help you cultivate a positive mindset:

Remember Strengths and Past Achievements. Remind yourself of your unique strengths and past successes. Focusing on your past achievements reinforces your confidence and helps you approach negotiations with a positive attitude.

Visualize Success. Visualization is a powerful tool for building confidence. Before entering a negotiation, take a few moments to visualize a successful outcome. Imagine yourself negotiating success-

---

1. The companion course for this book will contain a sample Negotiation Strategy document and much more. To sign up for the waiting list, visit https://bit.ly/nn-course

fully, overcoming challenges, and reaching a favorable agreement. Visualization prepares your mind for success.

Seek Support and Feedback

Having a support network can also boost your confidence and provide valuable perspectives. Surround yourself with people who can offer both encouragement and constructive feedback.

Here are some suggestions:

Build a Support Network. Find individuals within your professional network who can provide support and guidance. This could include colleagues, mentors, industry peers, or professional coaches. Reach out to them for advice and feedback on your negotiation strategies.

Peer Discussions. Join professional groups, forums, or associations where you can discuss negotiation strategies and experiences with peers. Engaging in peer discussions provides new perspectives and reinforces your confidence through shared learning.

Maintain Professionalism

When negotiating, it's easy to get thrown off balance when things aren't going as planned. However, confidence also stems from maintaining professionalism and composure, especially in challenging situations.

Here are some techniques that will help you to remain professional:

Stay Calm. Negotiations can become tense, but staying calm is crucial. Practice techniques to manage your emotions, such as deep breathing or taking brief pauses when needed. A calm demeanor projects confidence and control.

Assertive Communication. Communicate your points assertively and clearly. Avoid aggressive or passive language. Use confident body language, maintain eye contact, and speak with a steady tone. Assertive communication reinforces confidence and conveys authority.

Handle Objections Gracefully. Be prepared for objections and challenges during negotiations. Handle them gracefully by listening actively, acknowledging the other party's concerns, and responding with well-thought-out counterarguments. Handling objections professionally demonstrates your confidence and expertise.

By building confidence in your negotiating position, you enhance your ability to negotiate effectively. Confidence, combined with thorough preparation and a positive mindset, empowers you to assert your worth and navigate negotiations with poise and authority.

Okay, let's move on to communicating your value to the other party.

Communicate Your Value

Once you have a thorough understanding of your value and have built the confidence to assert your worth, the next crucial step is to communicate your value during negotiations. Clear communication ensures that the other party recognizes and respects your value.

"Value is what people are willing to pay for it."

— John Naisbitt

Craft a Clear Value Proposition

A well-crafted value proposition succinctly communicates the unique benefits you offer. It should be clear, concise, and tailored to your audience.

Consider these strategies:

Identify Key Benefits. Focus on the most compelling aspects of your product or service. Highlight what sets you apart from competitors and why the other party should choose you. Consider factors such as quality, innovation, reliability, and customer satisfaction.

Use Clear and Concise Language. Avoid jargon and complex language. Your value proposition should be easy to understand and memorable. Use straightforward language that clearly conveys your message.

Tailor Your Message. Customize your value proposition to address the other party's specific needs and concerns. Show how your product or service directly benefits them and solves their pain points. Personalization makes your message more relevant and persuasive.

Highlight Benefits and Differentiators

During negotiations, it's also essential to emphasize the benefits and unique aspects of your product or service. This helps the other party see the value you bring to the table.

Here are some ways to accomplish this:

Focus on Outcomes. Emphasize the positive outcomes and results the other party can expect by working with you. Highlight benefits such as cost savings, improved quality, or enhanced customer satisfaction.

Differentiate from Competitors. Articulate what makes you different from market competitors. Highlight your unique selling points and explain why these differentiators matter. Show how your product or service provides superior value compared to others in the market.

Address Pain Points. Identify and address the specific pain points and challenges the other party faces. Show how your offering can solve these problems and provide a better solution. Addressing pain points directly makes your value proposition much more compelling.

Use Data to Support Your Claims

Data and evidence are essential tools for reinforcing your value proposition. They provide objective proof that supports your claims and enhances your credibility.

Consider the following approaches:

Present Relevant Statistics: Use statistics that are directly relevant to the negotiation. This could include market share data, performance metrics, or customer satisfaction scores. Ensure that the data is accurate and timely.

Share Case Studies and Testimonials: Provide case studies and testimonials from satisfied customers. These real-world examples demonstrate how your product or service has delivered value to others. Make sure that the case studies highlight specific benefits and tangible results.

Share Independent Reviews and Endorsements: Independent (i.e., third-party) reviews and endorsements from reputable sources add credibility to your statements. Share positive reviews, awards, press releases, or certifications that validate your claims.

By effectively communicating your value to the other party, you can ensure that they fully understand and appreciate what you bring to the table.

Common Pitfalls to Avoid

Even with a thorough understanding of your worth and a well-prepared strategy, it's easy to fall into common pitfalls such as undervaluing or overvaluing your product or service. These mistakes can quickly undermine your negotiating position. By taking steps to avoid them, you can strengthen your negotiating approach.

Undervaluing Yourself

One of the most common mistakes in negotiations is undervaluing yourself. This can happen due to a lack of confidence, inadequate research, or a desire to reach an agreement quickly.

Here's how to avoid this pitfall:

Trust Your Research. Rely on the research you've conducted. Trust the data and evidence you've gathered about your market position and value. Use this information to back up your claims and stand firm when it comes to your worth.

Avoid Desperation. Never negotiate from a place of desperation. Even if the stakes are high, projecting confidence in your value is crucial. Desperation can lead to making unnecessary concessions and accepting unfavorable terms.

Overestimating Your Position

While confidence is key, overestimating your position can be just as detrimental. Overconfidence can lead to unrealistic demands and inflexibility, which can derail negotiations.

Here's how to maintain a balanced perspective:

Stay Grounded in Reality. Make sure that your demands are realistic and backed by solid evidence. Overconfidence can lead to making unreasonable requests that the other party is unlikely to accept.

Balance Confidence with Humility. Confidence should be tempered with humility. Acknowledge that while you bring significant value to the table, successful negotiations also require compromise and understanding. Always remember that the other party has alternatives too.

By avoiding these common pitfalls, you can increase the likelihood of a successful negotiation. A balanced approach will enable you to navigate these challenges confidently and successfully.

Key Takeaways

Understanding and asserting your worth is the cornerstone of successful negotiations. Throughout this chapter, we have explored the essential steps to recognize, evaluate, and communicate your value effectively. Knowing your worth allows you to negotiate from a position of strength, confidence, and clarity, which significantly improves your chances of achieving a favorable agreement.

Effective communication is key to ensuring that your value is recognized and respected. Crafting a compelling value proposition, convincingly presenting data and evidence, and handling objections professionally are all essential skills that reinforce your negotiating power. Clear and confident communication helps build trust and facilitates mutually beneficial agreements.

Building confidence in your negotiating position is equally crucial. You can develop the self-assurance needed to assert your worth effectively through preparation, practice, and a positive mindset. Engaging in role-playing exercises and seeking feedback from a supportive network further enhances your readiness for negotiations.

We also highlighted common pitfalls to avoid, such as undervaluing yourself and overestimating your position. By being aware of these traps and taking proactive steps to avoid them, you can maintain a strong negotiating stance and achieve better results.

By following this structured approach, you can ensure that you are well-prepared, confident, and ready to achieve your objectives. With the foundation of knowing your worth firmly in place, let's build on this knowledge and explore how to conduct thorough research.

CHAPTER 3
Do Your Homework

"Luck happens when preparation meets opportunity."

— Oprah Winfrey

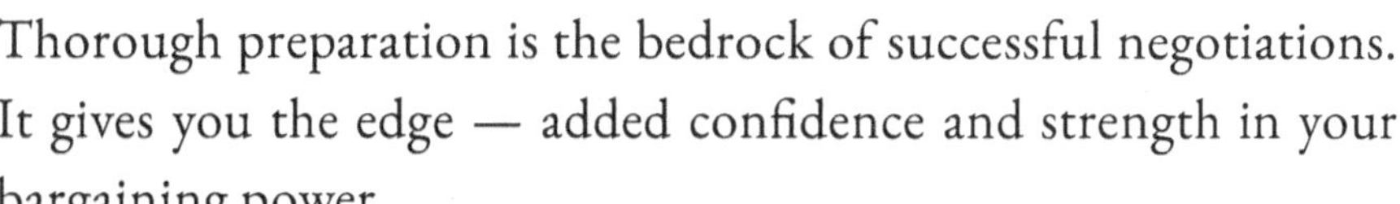

Thorough preparation is the bedrock of successful negotiations. It gives you the edge — added confidence and strength in your bargaining power.

While knowing your worth is crucial, being well-informed also improves your ability to secure better outcomes at the negotiating table. Thorough preparation not only enhances your credibility but also provides you with the insights to anticipate challenges, identify opportunities, and tailor your approach to meet the other party's specific needs. This can make the difference between a successful negotiation and a missed opportunity.

On the other hand, entering negotiations without adequate preparation exposes you to several risks that can significantly impact your success, such as:

Lack of Credibility. When you are not well-informed, it quickly becomes evident to the other party, which can diminish your credibility and weaken your negotiating position. The other party may perceive you as unprofessional or unprepared, making it harder to gain respect, trust, and concessions from the other party.

Reduced Negotiation Power. Thorough research provides the leverage needed to negotiate effectively. Without it, you lack the ability to support your arguments, making it challenging to justify your demands.

Increased Vulnerability. Unprepared negotiators are more vulnerable to pressure tactics and manipulation. The other party may exploit your lack of knowledge to push through their own agenda, leaving you at a severe disadvantage.

In this chapter, we will discuss the steps for conducting comprehensive research. We'll explore methods for collecting information about the other party, assessing their needs and limitations, and using that knowledge to strengthen your negotiation position. But first, let's start with gathering actionable insights, a.k.a. *"intelligence."*

Gathering Intelligence

Okay. Let's begin by level-setting what we mean by "intelligence." — No, this is not the type of intelligence generally associated with being smart or witty. This type of intelligence is more closely connected with military strategy:

> *Military intelligence is a military discipline that uses information collection and analysis approaches to provide guidance and direction to assist commanders in their decisions.*
>
> — Wikipedia

Planning to enter a serious negotiation begins with gathering comprehensive, accurate, and actionable information (i.e., *"intelligence"*). This foundational step equips you with the knowledge needed to understand the other party's position and potential leverage points.

To do this, you first need a deep understanding of the other party's needs, goals, and priorities. By understanding what drives the other party, you can tailor your approach to address their specific concerns, creating a more compelling case for your position.

Understand Priorities and Motivations

Identifying the priorities and motivations of the other party allows you to create proposals that align with their interests.

Here's how to do this:

Identify Key Decision Makers. It's important to know the organization's key decision-makers. Understanding their roles, responsibilities, and stakeholders can help you tailor your approach to address specific concerns rather than general ideas.

Assess Business Goals. Look for information on the other party's business goals and objectives. This might include growth targets, market expansion plans, cost reduction initiatives, or quality improvement efforts. Aligning your proposal with their strategic goals increases the likelihood of a positive response.

Understand Their Pain Points. Identify the challenges and pain points the other party is facing. Offering solutions to these pain points can make your proposal more attractive.

Review Their History and Reputation

A thorough understanding of the other party's negotiation history and reputation can help you anticipate their strategies and behaviors.

Here's how to gather this information:

Use Previous Negotiations. If you have knowledge about the other party's previous negotiations, review the outcomes and the corresponding strategies they employed. This can provide insights into their negotiation style, common tactics, and potential red lines.

Know their Reputation. Research the other party's reputation within the industry. Are they known for being fair and collaborative, or are they perceived as tough negotiators? Industry forums, trade associations, and peer networks may provide valuable information.

Use Insights to Strengthen Your Bargaining Position

Once you have gathered detailed information about the other party's needs, goals, and constraints, use this knowledge to strengthen your negotiation position.

Consider these strategies:

Tailor Your Proposal. Customize your proposal to address the other party's specific needs and priorities. Highlight how your offer aligns with their goals and solves their main pain points. A tailored proposal demonstrates that you have done your homework and are committed to a mutually beneficial agreement.

Anticipate Objections. Use the information you've gathered to anticipate potential objections and prepare counterarguments. Addressing concerns proactively shows that you understand their perspective and are prepared to work towards a solution.

Understand Their Negotiating Style. Negotiators typically adopt one of five distinct styles (i.e., Competitive, Collaborative, Comprising, Avoiding, or Accommodating), each with its own characteristics and strategies. By understanding the other party, you can approach negotiations with a well-informed, strategic perspective.[1]

Assess Your Strengths, Weaknesses & Bargaining Position

A thorough, pragmatic analysis of your strengths and weaknesses is also essential for effective negotiation. Knowing where you excel and where you might be vulnerable will help you maximize your advantages and mitigate potential risks.

---

1. In the companion course, we discuss the 5 negotiating styles and cxplain how to recognize and adapt to each strategy. If you'd like to be notified when we launch the course, go to https://bit.ly/nn-course

Evaluate Your Strengths

Begin by evaluating your key strengths, which set you apart from the competition.

Consider the following areas:

Product/Service Quality. Assess the quality of your products or services compared to competitors. Highlight unique features, superior craftsmanship, or innovative elements that distinguish what you have to offer.

Brand Reputation. Consider your brand's reputation in the market. Strong brand recognition and positive customer feedback can be significant assets. Gather testimonials, industry awards, and media mentions that reinforce your brand's strength.

Operational Efficiency. Examine your operational processes for efficiency and reliability. Consistent delivery times, low defect rates, and effective supply chain management are indicators of operational strength.

Financial Health. Assess your financial position, including profitability, revenue growth, and cash flow stability. Strong financial health enhances your negotiating power by demonstrating stability and reliability.

Identify Your Weaknesses

Understanding your weaknesses is equally important, as it allows you to address potential vulnerabilities and prepare for challenges.

Here are some key areas that you'll want to focus on:

Product/Service Limitations. Identify any limitations or areas where your products or services fall short compared to competitors. Consider quality issues, lack of features, or negative customer feedback.

Brand Challenges. Assess any brand-related challenges, including past negative publicity or market perception issues, that could undermine your position.

Operational Inefficiencies. Examine your operational processes for inefficiencies or bottlenecks. Missed deadlines, high defect rates, or supply chain disruptions can be significant weaknesses in negotiations.

Financial Constraints. Evaluate any financial constraints or weaknesses, such as declining revenue, high debt levels, or cash flow problems. These issues can limit your flexibility and bargaining power.

Resource Limitations. Consider any limitations in resources, such as manpower, technology, or expertise. Limited resources can affect your ability to meet demands or deliver on promises, which, if discovered, may undermine your negotiation position.

Analyze the Impact on Negotiations

After identifying your strengths and weaknesses, the next step is to consider their impact on your negotiation strategy.

Here's how to approach this analysis:

Strengths — First, determine how each strength enhances your negotiation position. Quantify the benefits of your strengths where possible, using metrics and data to support your claims.

Weaknesses — Next, assess the potential risks and challenges associated with each weakness. Consider how the other party might perceive these weaknesses and anticipate potential objections. Develop strategies to mitigate or downplay these weaknesses, such as proposing solutions, offering reassurances, or focusing on other strengths to compensate.

Understand Market Conditions

Market conditions can significantly alter the tone of any negotiation. They influence the dynamics of supply and demand, pricing strategies, and competitive behavior. By analyzing these conditions, you can better anticipate challenges and opportunities, tailor your approach, and make informed decisions.

Analyze Current Trends

Market trends give insights into the direction of your specific industry. Keeping up with these trends allows you to align your strategy with current and future market conditions.

Here are some things to look for:

Identify Key Trends. Look for major movements that are shaping your industry. These could include technological advancements, shifts in consumer preferences, regulatory changes, and economic factors. Use industry reports, market analysis, and news articles to stay informed.

Evaluate Impact on Your Business. Consider how these trends impact your business and the negotiation context. For example, if there is a growing demand for sustainable products, highlight your commitment to sustainability as a key strength.

Forecast Future Developments. Finally, use trend analysis to forecast future market developments. Anticipating future changes allows you to stay ahead of competitors.

Know the Economic and Regulatory Climate

Economic and regulatory factors can significantly impact market conditions and negotiations. Staying informed about these factors ensures that you are prepared for any external influences.

Consider the following factors:

Economic Indicators. Monitor key economic indicators such as inflation rates, interest rates, market growth, and unemployment rates. These indicators provide insights into the overall economic environment and its direct (or indirect) impact on your industry.

Regulatory Changes. Stay up-to-date on regulatory changes that affect your industry. This includes new or changing laws, regulations, and compliance requirements. Understanding the regulatory environment helps you anticipate sudden changes and challenges while remaining compliant with legal requirements.

Global Considerations. Consider the impact of global factors such as trade policies, international competition, and geopolitical conflicts (i.e., wars, coups, embargos). Global events can quickly influence market conditions and create opportunities or challenges for your business.

The Dynamics of Supply and Demand

Supply and demand dynamics also play a crucial role in negotiations. Understanding these dynamics helps you gauge the market's capacity and identify opportunities to leverage your position.

Here's how to analyze supply and demand:

Supply Analysis. Evaluate the supply side of the market, including the availability of key resources, production capacities, and supplier reliability. Identify any potential supply chain disruptions or bottlenecks that could impact negotiations.

Demand Analysis. Assess the demand side by examining customer needs, market size, and growth potential. Look for emerging trends in customer preferences and purchasing behavior. Use customer surveys, sales data, and market research to gather key insights.

Balance of Power. Determine the balance of power between supply and demand. In markets with high demand and limited supply, sellers have more leverage. Conversely, in markets with plenty of supply and lower demand, buyers hold more negotiating power. Use this to tailor your negotiation strategy accordingly.

Assess the Competitive Landscape

Understanding your competition provides additional context for your positioning and helps you understand how to differentiate yourself. Carefully analyzing your competitors allows you to identify your unique strengths and weaknesses relative to others in the market.

Consider these strategies:

Recognize Key Competitors. List your main competitors, focusing on those that operate in the same market segment and target similar customer bases. Gather information on their products, services, pricing, and marketing strategies.

Benchmark Performance. Compare your market performance against that of your competitors. Identify areas where you excel and areas where you may lag behind the competition. Use this analysis to highlight your competitive advantages and address any gaps.

Monitor Competitor Behavior. Track your competitors' actions, such as new product launches, marketing campaigns, and strategic partnerships. Understanding their strategies helps you anticipate their future moves.

The Power of Networking

Networking is a powerful (yet often understated) method of gathering information, gaining insights, and enhancing your negotiation strategy. I often like to think of networking as *"boots on the ground,"* which, in a pragmatic sense, means talking to the people who are actually doing the work. Building a robust network of industry contacts and professional associations can provide you with valuable resources and perspectives that are not always accessible online.

Here are some tips to build and maintain a valuable network:

Attend Industry Events: Conferences, trade shows, seminars, and workshops relevant to your industry provide great opportunities to meet potential contacts, learn about the latest trends, and gain insights from experts.

Join Professional Associations. Consider joining professional associations related to your field. These organizations often provide networking opportunities, resources, and events that can help you connect with industry peers and experts.

Reach Out Directly. Don't hesitate to reach out to potential contacts via email or social media. Introduce yourself, explain why you are reaching out, and suggest a meeting or call to discuss common interests.

Follow-Up. After initial contact, follow up to maintain the relationship. Share relevant information, congratulate them on their achievements, or simply check in periodically.

By building a network of industry contacts and leveraging professional associations and groups, you can validate and enhance your research efforts, gain valuable insights, and broaden your skills. Networking provides access to information, resources, and support that are crucial for successful negotiations.

Use Market Conditions in Negotiations

Leveraging your understanding of market conditions can further enhance your bargaining power.

Here's how to integrate this knowledge into your negotiation strategy:

Align with Trends. Tailor your proposals to align with current market trends. Emphasize how your products or services meet the latest consumer demands or leverage new technologies. Demonstrating a deep understanding of market trends makes your proposals more relevant and appealing.

Use Supply and Demand Dynamics. Use your knowledge of supply and demand to strengthen your bargaining position. If you have a scarce resource in a high-demand market, emphasize its value. Conversely, if you are negotiating in a buyer's market, use competitive pricing and value-added services to differentiate yourself.

Differentiate from Competitors. Highlight your unique strengths and competitive advantages. Use benchmarking data to show how you provide better value than your competitors. Market differentiation reinforces your position and increases your appeal.

Approaching negotiations with a well-informed perspective not only enhances your credibility but also allows you to make strategic decisions that maximize your advantages and address potential challenges during negotiation.

Common Pitfalls to Avoid

Several common mistakes should be avoided when preparing for negotiations. These include failing to do enough research, not understanding the data (or using it incorrectly), allowing biases and assumptions to lead to faulty conclusions, and overlooking important details critical to the negotiating process.

Let's start with insufficient research.

Insufficient Research

Failing to conduct adequate research can undermine your position, reduce your credibility, and lead to unfavorable results. To avoid the pitfalls of insufficient research, consider these best practices:

Allocate Sufficient Time. Before entering negotiations, allot enough time for thorough research. Start your preparation early to avoid last-minute rushes and incomplete information.

Set Clear Research Objectives. Based on your negotiation goals, identify the key areas you need to explore, such as market conditions, competitor analysis, and potential leverage points.

Use Reliable Sources. Rely on credible sources. Verify the accuracy and currency of the information you gather against multiple sources to ensure its validity.

Seek Expert Insights. When dealing with complex topics or unfamiliar industries, seek insights from experts or consultants. Their specialized knowledge can provide a deeper understanding and enhance your preparation.

Stay Updated. Market conditions and industry trends can change rapidly. Stay updated by regularly reviewing industry reports, news articles, and other relevant sources. Continuous learning is crucial for maintaining an informed perspective.

Prepare for Different Scenarios. Anticipate various negotiation scenarios and prepare responses for each. Consider the possible objections, counteroffers, and challenges you might face, and how to address them.

Misinterpreting Data

Accurate data analysis is critical to forming sound negotiation strategies. Misinterpreting data can lead to incorrect conclusions, poor decision-making, and a weakened negotiating position.

Here are some ways to ensure that data is interpreted correctly:

Check for Consistency. Regularly check for consistency within your data sets. Inconsistent data can indicate errors or inaccuracies. Use statistical methods to identify outliers and anomalies that may require further investigation.

Apply the Correct Methodologies. Ensure that you apply the correct methodologies for your analysis. Misapplication of methods can lead to incorrect results. If necessary, consult with experts or use industry-standard guidelines to select the appropriate methodologies.

Review and Revise. After completing your analysis, review your findings carefully. Rethink both your data and methodology to ensure that your conclusions are well-supported.

Avoiding Biases and Assumptions

Biases and assumptions are one of the most dangerous shortcomings of business. They undermine negotiations by distorting facts, generally leading to faulty conclusions.

Here's are some strategies for avoiding them:

Recognize Common Bias Types: Be aware of common biases, such as confirmation bias (i.e., *favoring information that confirms pre-existing beliefs*), selection bias (i.e., *choosing non-representative samples*), and anchoring bias (i.e., *relying too heavily on initial information*). Understanding these biases helps you identify and counteract them.

Use Objective Criteria: Base your analysis on objective criteria rather than subjective opinions or assumptions. Develop clear, measurable criteria for evaluating data and making decisions. This assures that your analysis is grounded in factual evidence.

Get a Different Opinion. Involve multiple stakeholders in the analysis process to bring diverse perspectives and reduce individual biases. Challenge assumptions to uncover potential blind spots.

Document Assumptions Made. Clearly document any assumptions you make during your analysis. Explain the rationale behind these assumptions and consider their potential impact on your findings. This can help you evaluate their validity and adjust if needed.

By ensuring accuracy in data analysis and avoiding biases and assumptions, you can form well-supported conclusions that support your negotiation strategy. Accurate data analysis provides a solid foundation for decision-making, helping you approach negotiations with clarity.

Overlooking Important Details

Thorough research and attention to detail are also crucial in negotiations. Overlooking important details can lead to misunderstandings and costly mistakes. Double-checking your information is essential to ensure accuracy and avoid errors that could undermine your negotiation efforts.

Here are some tips to systematically verify your data:

Review Data Sources. Revisit the original sources of your data to ensure that the information is accurate and up-to-date. Remember Moore's Law (i.e., technology capability doubles every 5 years). Verify the credibility and reliability of each source.

Detail-Oriented Review. Conduct a detailed review of all collected data, reports, and analyses. Look for inconsistencies, errors, or omissions. Pay attention to small details that could have a significant impact on the negotiation.

Conduct a Peer Review. Have colleagues or team members review your research and findings. A fresh set of eyes can catch errors you might have missed and provide additional insights.

Perform Scenario Analysis. Conduct scenario analysis to test your data under different conditions. This helps ensure that your information holds up in various contexts and is not based on overly optimistic or pessimistic assumptions.

Documentation. Keep detailed records of your research process, sources, and findings. Documentation allows you to trace back and verify information if questions arise during negotiations.

By conducting thorough research, you can ensure that you are well-prepared for negotiations. This approach enhances your ability to make informed decisions, respond effectively to challenges, and helps tilt the odds in your favor.

Key Takeaways

Preparation is essential to successful negotiation. As we have explored throughout this chapter, preparation provides the knowledge, confidence, and strategic insight needed during the negotiation process. By investing time and effort into detailed research, you can anticipate potential challenges, understand the other party's needs and constraints, and develop a comprehensive negotiation strategy. Preparation is not just about gathering information but also analyzing, synthesizing, and applying this information effectively.

Your research provides a solid foundation for informed decision-making and effective negotiation. Showing a deep understanding of relevant facts and trends builds your credibility. It proves that you are well-prepared and serious about reaching a successful agreement.

Accurate and up-to-date information allows you to evaluate offers, assess risks, and identify opportunities with greater precision. Thus, you reduce the likelihood of surprises and enhance your ability to manage risks effectively. This, in turn, also helps you identify leverage points and develop strategies that align with your objectives.

Finally, being well-prepared boosts your confidence and clarity during negotiations. You can articulate your points more effectively, respond to challenges confidently, and navigate the negotiation process with ease.

In summary, thorough preparation and research are indispensable. They provide the knowledge, insights, and strategic advantages needed to achieve your goals and build strong, collaborative relationships with the other party. By prioritizing preparation, you set the stage for success.

Let's move on to one of the most important aspects of becoming a negotiation ninja — listening more than you speak.

CHAPTER 4
Listen More Than You Speak

"Most of the successful people I've known are the ones who do more listening than talking."
— Bernard Baruch

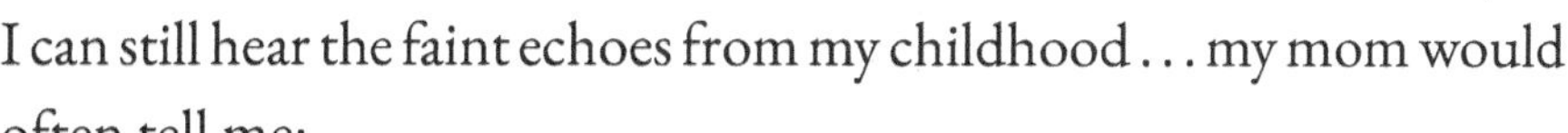

I can still hear the faint echoes from my childhood . . . my mom would often tell me:

". . . Boy, there's a reason why God gave you only one mouth, but two ears. Use them. Be quiet and listen."

Thanks, Mom.

Over the years, I gradually understood those powerful words. Sadly, listening is undervalued in our modern "me-first" society. In a world where everyone wants to be heard, very few actually take the time to listen carefully to what others have to say.

Listening is an important skill in business, but it's even more critical in negotiations. While presenting your case is important, the ability to listen effectively often determines the ultimate success of a negotiation. Listening allows you to truly understand the other party's needs, concerns, and motivations, which is essential for discovering what works for both parties.

Listening is not just about physically hearing the words being spoken; it involves actively engaging with the speaker, interpreting their overt (i.e., apparent, obvious) and covert (i.e., concealed, hidden) messaging,[1] and responding with purpose and intent. Effective listening can transform a negotiation from a competitive battle into a collaborative effort, leading to better results.

Throughout the negotiating process, listening serves several key purposes. First, it demonstrates respect for the other party's views. Second, it provides a deeper understanding of the other party's priorities, constraints, and underlying interests. Third, it helps uncover areas of mutual agreement and shared goals, encouraging collaboration and compromise.

Negotiation ninjas don't just listen to gather information. They listen to lay a foundation for productive negotiation. Mastering the art

---

1. According to experts, *"Studies have quoted figures from 50% to 90% that communication—the message and emotion we get from others—is based on nonverbal or unspoken signals."* This suggests that covert signals convey the real meaning that the speaker is communicating. See, e.g., "Overt and Covert Communication" https://newtonmg.com/2020/09/06/overt-and-covert-communication/

of listening will significantly improve your ability to reach favorable deals while building lasting relationships.

What Active Listening Really Entails

Throughout this book, we've discussed active listening extensively. But now, it's time to examine what it really means.

Active listening is a communication technique that involves fully engaging with the speaker, understanding their message, and responding thoughtfully. It goes beyond just hearing the words being spoken; it requires conscious effort to comprehend the speaker's perspective, emotions, and underlying motivations.

Let's take a step back to examine the process of active listening and then contrast this to mere passive listening.

The 4-Step Process of Active Listening

As illustrated below, here are the 4 steps of active listening, along with a brief definition for each:

STEP 1: Receiving. Actively focus on the speaker, avoiding distractions and showing through your body language that you are attentive.

STEP 2: Understanding. Interpret the message by considering the speaker's words, tone, and body language. Look for underlying emotions and intentions.

STEP 3: Evaluating. Judge the content of the message without jumping to conclusions. Consider the information objectively and reflect on its implications.

STEP 4: Responding. Provide feedback to the speaker to confirm understanding. This could involve summarizing what was said, asking clarifying questions, or expressing empathy.

Active Listening vs. Passive Listening

In contrast to active listening, passive listening involves just hearing the words without fully engaging with or understanding the speaker. Passive listeners might nod or give brief acknowledgments, but they do not invest the mental energy to truly comprehend the speaker's message, acknowledge the points, or respond meaningfully.

Recognizing a Passive Listener

Passive listeners are mentally and emotionally disconnected from the speaker. They often appear distracted or disinterested, failing to provide feedback or ask questions. Quite often, they only invest enough energy to gain a surface-level understanding of the message being conveyed.

Passive listeners might hear the words, but often miss the deeper meaning, emotions, and context behind the message. Finally, they have minimal interaction with the speaker, offering vague or limited responses, usually just enough to keep the conversation going without any significant contribution.

4 Differences Between Active and Passive Listening

1. ***Attention.*** Active listening involves full attention and focus on the speaker, while passive listening can involve divided attention and distractions.

2. ***Engagement.*** Active listeners engage with the speaker, reflecting and responding thoughtfully, whereas passive listeners provide minimal feedback.

3. ***Comprehension.*** Active listeners strive to understand the full message, including emotions and context, while passive listeners may only grasp the superficial meaning (or none at all).

4. Interaction. Active listening fosters a two-way dialogue with meaningful exchanges, while passive listening often results in a one-sided conversation.

"Wisdom is the reward you get for a lifetime of listening when you'd have preferred to talk."
— Doug Larson

Active Listening Techniques

Now that we know what active listening involves and how it differs from passive listening let's look at some practical active listening techniques. Specifically, we'll examine what it means to give the speaker your full attention, reflect and paraphrase, ask open-ended questions, and pick up on nonverbal cues.

Give Your Full Attention

Active listening begins with giving the speaker your full attention. This involves eliminating distractions and focusing completely on the speaker's words and body language. By doing so, you show respect and demonstrate that you value what the speaker has to say.

Start by eliminating distractions by choosing a suitable location free from noise and interruptions. Silence your phone and other electronic devices that might interrupt the flow of the conversation. Before the meeting, take a mindfulness moment to clear your mind of other thoughts and concerns. This mental preparation helps you stay present and attentive during the conversation.

You create a respectful and focused environment that facilitates more productive negotiations by giving the other party your full attention. This sets the stage for more effective communication and collaboration.

Reflect and Paraphrase

Reflecting and paraphrasing also promote mutual understanding during negotiations. Paraphrasing involves restating the speaker's message in your own words. This helps verify that you have correctly understood their points and allows the speaker to correct any misunderstandings.

Summarizing involves condensing the speaker's key points into a brief overview. This technique is particularly useful for longer discussions, as it helps clarify the main issues and ensures that both parties are aligned. For example, *"To summarize, you're facing challenges with . . . Is that an accurate summary of your concerns?"*

Reflecting the speaker's emotions also involves acknowledging and validating their feelings. This demonstrates empathy and helps build a stronger connection. For example, *"It sounds like you're feeling frustrated with the current process. I understand that this has been a difficult experience for you."*

Ask Open-ended Questions

Open-ended questions encourage detailed responses and help uncover the other party's underlying interests and concerns. By asking these types of questions, you gain deeper insights and enhance mutual understanding.

Open-ended questions are designed to elicit more than just a 'yes' or 'no' answer. They encourage the speaker to provide detailed information, share their thoughts, and elaborate on their views.

Start questions with ***"What,"*** ***"How,"*** ***"Why,"*** or ***"Can you explain..."***:

These types of question starters prompt the speaker to think more deeply and provide comprehensive responses. For example: *"How do you envision . . . ?" or "What are your main concerns regarding . . . ?"*

Examples of Effective Open-ended Questions

- ***Understanding Needs . . .*** *"**What** are the most important factors for you in this negotiation?"*
- ***Exploring Options . . .*** *"**How** do you think we can address this issue together?"*
- ***Clarifying Motivations . . .*** *"**Why** is this particular term significant for you?"*
- ***Seeking Feedback . . .*** *"**Can you explain** how this proposal aligns with your goals?"*

Additionally, use open-ended questions to understand the underlying interests and motivations behind the other party's stated position. This helps you understand what truly matters to them. For example, if the other party demands a specific price, ask, *"What factors are driving your need for this price point?"*

By asking open-ended questions that encourage detailed responses and using these questions to explore underlying interests and concerns, you can gain deeper insights into the other party's perspective. This enables you to tailor your proposals more effectively and promote a more collaborative and productive negotiation process.

Look for Non-Verbal Cues

Non-verbal communication also plays a significant role in active listening. It includes body language, facial expressions, eye contact, gestures, and tone of voice. Understanding and using non-verbal cues can enhance your ability to listen and respond appropriately during negotiations.

Consider these suggestions:

Read Body Language. The way someone sits or stands can indicate their level of comfort, confidence, and openness. Open postures (e.g., uncrossed arms, leaning slightly forward) suggest engagement and receptivity, while closed postures (e.g., crossed arms, leaning back) may indicate defensiveness or discomfort.

Gestures. Hand movements and other gestures can provide additional context to verbal communication. Pay attention to how gestures align with the speaker's words to gauge sincerity and emphasis.

Microexpressions. These brief, involuntary facial expressions can reveal true emotions that might be hidden. They are quick but can provide deep insight into a person's genuine feelings. For example, A fleeting look of frustration or surprise might indicate underlying concerns that haven't been verbally expressed.

Avoiding Negative Signals. Finally, be mindful of your own nonverbal signals that might convey frustration, discontent, or negativity, such as fidgeting, checking your watch, or rolling your eyes. These actions can undermine your verbal message.

By effectively interpreting the other party's non-verbal cues and using your own non-verbal signals to show engagement, you can enhance communication and build stronger connections during the negotiating process.

Handling Tense Situations

Negotiations can quickly become emotionally charged, especially when the stakes are high because parties have competing interests. Managing your emotions is the key to maintaining a productive negotiation environment.

First, stay calm. Practicing deep breathing exercises can help reduce anxiety and maintain calmness. Slow, deep breaths help lower your heart rate and clear your mind. If you feel emotions rising, take a second to pause before answering. This brief moment of mindful reflection allows you to stop, gather your thoughts, and choose a more deliberate response.

It is also important to keep your goals in mind. Remind yourself of the overall objectives and desired outcomes of the negotiation. Focusing on your goals can help you stay grounded and prevent emotional reactions from derailing the discussion. Additionally, keep your tone of voice neutral and composed, even if you feel frustrated or angry. A calm tone helps de-escalate tension. Finally, be aware of physical signs of tension, such as clenched fists or tight shoulders, and consciously relax those areas. A relaxed body helps promote a calm mind.

Use Emotional Intelligence

Emotional intelligence (or, E.I.) refers to the ability to recognize, understand, manage, and utilize emotions effectively in oneself and others. It encompasses skills such as emotional awareness, empathy, self-regulation, and social skills, which are crucial for building relationships, navigating complex social situations, and making informed decisions.

Here are some ways to leverage this during negotiations:

Be self-aware. Being aware of your own emotions and those of others is the first step in managing them effectively. Recognize when raw emotions are influencing the negotiation and take steps to address them. For example, If you sense that frustration is building on both sides, acknowledge it and suggest a short break to allow everyone to regroup.

Understand Their Perspective. Show empathy by trying to understand the other party's emotions and viewpoints. Empathy can help build rapport and reduce tension. For instance, If the other party seems upset, acknowledge their feelings: *"I understand that this issue is very important to you, and I want to find a solution that works for both of us."*

Always Stay in Control. Control your emotions to prevent them from negatively impacting the negotiation. Techniques like deep breathing, positive self-talk, and taking breaks can help you maintain control.

Express Emotions Constructively. When necessary, express your emotions in a constructive manner. Use "I" statements to communicate how you feel without blaming or accusing the other party. For example: *"I feel concerned about... because it might impact our ability to deliver..."*

Use De-escalation Techniques. Use techniques to de-escalate tension, such as speaking in a calm tone, acknowledging the other party's concerns, and finding common ground. For instance, If the conversation becomes heated, lower your voice, slow down your speech, and express a desire to work collaboratively: *"Let's take a step back and find a solution that addresses both of our concerns."*

Stay Solution-oriented. Focus on finding solutions rather than dwelling on problems. This positive approach can help defuse emotions and keep the negotiation on track. For example, instead of getting stuck on points of contention, redirect the conversation towards potential solutions: *"What can we do to overcome this obstacle together?"*

By managing emotions and staying calm, you can navigate difficult negotiations more effectively, maintain a constructive atmosphere, and work towards mutually beneficial outcomes. Emotional intelligence plays a crucial role in understanding and regulating both your emotions and those of others, leading to more productive and positive discussions.

Handling Interruptions and Distractions

In addition to keeping your emotions in check, handling interruptions is also critical to productive negotiation. Interruptions and distractions can derail negotiations, making it difficult to focus. Managing disruptions is vital to keeping the negotiation on track and ensuring that all parties remain engaged.

Consider the following tips for handling interruptions and distractions:

Establish Ground Rules. At the beginning of the negotiation, agree on ground rules to minimize interruptions and distractions. This includes turning off mobile phones, avoiding side conversations, and respecting speaking turns. For example: *"I want to ensure that everyone is heard and we have a productive negotiation today. Let's agree to keep our phones on silent and avoid using them during our discussion to stay focused."*

Consider The Environment. Choose a quiet, comfortable location for the negotiation, free from external distractions such as noise and traffic. Ensure the setting is conducive to focused discussion.

Use an Agenda for a Structured Discussion. Develop and share an agenda before the meeting to provide structure and keep the discussion on track. Refer to the agenda if the conversation starts to veer off course. For example: *"According to our agenda, we need to address . . . next. Let's refocus on that point."*

Summarize and Refocus. Periodically summarize key points to refocus the discussion and ensure everyone is on the same page. This technique helps redirect the conversation if it starts to stray. For example: *"To summarize, we've agreed on . . . but still need to finalize . . . Let's continue with that."*

Handle Interruptions Politely but Acknowledge and Redirect. If someone interrupts, acknowledge their point briefly and suggest returning to the main topic. This keeps the discussion on track without dismissing the interrupter's input. For example: *"That's an* *important point, and I'd like to address it after we finish discussing the timeline."*

Take Breaks to Avoid Fatigue. Schedule regular breaks to prevent fatigue and maintain focus. Breaks provide an opportunity to regroup and return to the negotiation with renewed concentration.

Acknowledge and Move Forward. If a distraction occurs, address it directly and then steer the conversation back to the main topic. For example: *"I understand your concern about... We'll cover that shortly, but let's finish discussing... first."*

Use Transition Phrases. Employ transition phrases to smoothly guide the conversation back to the main topic after an interruption. For example: *"Getting back to our discussion on . . . , let's review the proposed terms."*

Use Clarifying Questions to Refocus Attention. Clarifying questions bring the conversation back to the main points and ensure all parties are aligned. For example, *"Can we clarify how this impacts our agreed-upon term of... ?"*

Reiterate Primary Goals. Remind everyone of the negotiation's objectives to refocus the discussion and emphasize the importance of staying on track. For example: *"Our main goal today is to finalize ... Let's ensure we address that before moving on to other topics."*

Periodically Recap. Provide regular summaries of the discussion to keep everyone focused and ensure that all key points are addressed. For example: *"So far, we've agreed on... Next, let's discuss..."*

Maintain a Positive Tone. When redirecting the conversation, use a positive and collaborative tone to encourage cooperation and minimize resistance. For example, *"I appreciate your input on . . . Let's make sure we finish the current discussion so we can give . . . the attention it deserves."*

By implementing these strategies, you can effectively handle interruptions and distractions, ensuring that the negotiation remains productive and focused. Maintaining focus not only enhances the efficiency of the negotiation process but also helps build trust and cooperation among all parties involved.

Managing Aggressive or Uncooperative Behavior

When one party exhibits aggressive or uncooperative behavior, it can make for an extremely challenging negotiation. If this happens and you still deem the negotiation worth continuing, it is important to know how to manage this conduct.

Here are some suggestions:

Set Boundaries. Clearly establish boundaries and acceptable behavior at the outset of the negotiation. This helps prevent aggressive or uncooperative behavior from disrupting the process. For example: *"I understand that this is a sensitive issue, but let's agree to keep our discussion respectful and focused on finding a solution."*

Avoid Escalation. Use neutral, non-confrontational language to avoid escalating the situation. This helps keep the conversation productive and reduces the likelihood of further aggression. For example: Instead of saying, *"You're being unreasonable,"* try, *"Let's explore other options that might address your concerns."*

Redirect Negative Behavior. When faced with aggressive or uncooperative behavior, redirect the conversation back to the issues and away from personal attacks or negative comments. For example: *"I hear your frustration. Let's focus on how we can move forward and find a solution that works for both of us."*

Pause to De-escalate. If the situation becomes too heated, suggest taking a short break to allow everyone to cool down and regain composure.

Remain Firm but Fair. Be assertive in expressing your needs and boundaries, but remain fair and open to the other party's concerns. This balance can help manage difficult behavior while maintaining a productive dialogue. For example: *"I understand your concerns, but I need us to stay focused on the agenda we agreed upon to ensure we cover all the necessary points."*

Find Areas of Agreement. Look for areas where you can agree, even if they are small. Finding common ground can help build rapport and reduce uncooperative behavior. For example: *"We both want this project to succeed. Let's work together to address the challenges we're facing."*

Maintain Professionalism. Keep your demeanor professional at all times, regardless of the other party's behavior. This sets a positive example and helps maintain a respectful negotiation environment. Respond to personal attacks or insults with professionalism and redirect the conversation to the relevant issues.

Suggest a Mediator or Neutral Third Party. If aggressive or uncooperative behavior continues to disrupt the negotiation, consider involving a neutral mediator to salvage the discussion and help manage conflicts. For example: *"It seems like we're having trouble finding common ground. Would it be helpful to bring in a mediator to assist us in reaching an agreement?"*

By using these techniques to listen effectively to challenging individuals and manage aggressive or uncooperative behavior, you can maintain control of the negotiation process and focus on achieving productive results. Handling difficult personalities with composure and professionalism helps ensure a positive and collaborative negotiation.

Common Pitfalls to Avoid

When it comes to listening, there are 3 common pitfalls that derail negotiations. Specifically, interrupting the other party, making assumptions about what is being said or the meaning behind it, and focusing on your own response instead of focusing on the speaker.

Let's examine each of these and see how to avoid them.

Interrupting the Speaker

Interrupting the speaker during negotiations can undermine the negotiation process and stifle effective communication. It signals a lack of respect and consideration for the other party's perspective, which can damage trust and weaken the personal connection needed for successful negotiations.

It also hinders understanding by preventing the speaker from fully expressing their thoughts. This leads to incomplete information and misunderstandings, which can undermine problem-solving and decision-making.

Finally, frequent interruptions can escalate tension and frustration, making the negotiation environment more adversarial. This can lead to unnecessary conflicts and reduce the likelihood of reaching a mutually beneficial agreement.

How to Avoid Cutting Off the Other Party

First, remember to be patient and wait for the speaker to finish before responding. This shows respect and ensures you have all the information needed to respond effectively.

Second, take notes during the discussion to capture key points and questions you want to address. This helps you remember your points without needing to interrupt. Once the speaker has finished, reflect back and summarize their key points to confirm understanding before presenting your response. For example: *"I understand that your main concern is... Let's discuss how we can address that."*

IMPORTANT NINJA TIP: At the start of the negotiation, it is totally okay to establish ground rules that include allowing each party to speak without interruption. This sets a respectful tone for the discussion. For instance, *"Let's agree to let each person finish their point before responding to ensure everyone is heard."*

During the conversation, if you need more information or clarification, wait until the speaker has finished and then ask open-ended questions to encourage further elaboration. For example: *"Can you provide more details about the challenges you're facing with . . . ?"*

Finally, remember to use active and reflective listening techniques to validate your understanding. Summarize and reflect back what the speaker has said, showing that you listened and understood before making your point. For example: *"It sounds like you're concerned about . . . Let's explore some options to address that."*

By allowing the speaker to express their thoughts, you help maintain a more respectful, productive, and collaborative negotiation, which ultimately improves the chances of reaching a successful agreement.

IMPORTANT NINJA TIP: Work on developing your self-awareness. Self-awareness will improve your communication skills. If you notice yourself getting ready to interrupt, pause, take a deep breath, and remind yourself to listen before responding.

Making Assumptions

Making assumptions during negotiations can lead to misunderstandings, miscommunications, and missed opportunities. Assumptions often lead to incorrect conclusions about intentions, needs, or goals. This can result in decisions based on false premises.

"Assumptions are the termites of relationships."
— Henry Winkler

When you assume you understand without asking for clarification, you risk overlooking important details that could impact the negotiation. Even worse, assumptions can escalate into conflicts, making it harder to reach a final agreement.

Tips to Avoid Making Assumptions

First, don't be afraid to explicitly state your assumptions and ask the other party to confirm or correct them. This ensures that your understanding aligns with their intentions. For example: *"I assume that you prefer to . . . because of . . . Is that accurate?"*

As the negotiations progress, continue to use clarifying questions to verify your understanding of the other party's points and concerns. This ensures all relevant information is considered. For example: *"Can you clarify what you mean by . . . ? Are there specific conditions you're thinking of?"*

If any part of the discussion is unclear or ambiguous, ask for clarification to prevent assumptions from filling in the gaps. For example: *"You mentioned that . . . is critical. Can you specify the exact constraints you're working with?"*

Finally, encourage the other party to provide feedback on your understanding of the issues. This will allow them to elaborate and clarify their position. For example, *"Please let me know if I've misunderstood any part of your proposal. I want to make sure we're on the same page."*

IMPORTANT NINJA TIP: Keep written records of the key points and agreements reached during the negotiation. This will provide a reference point to ensure a consistent understanding among all parties.

By avoiding assumptions, you can enhance communication, build trust, and create a more effective negotiation environment. Clarity and mutual understanding prevent conflicts, fosters collaboration, and leads to better results.

Focusing on Your Own Response

Another common pitfall that commonly derails negotiations is focusing too much on your own response rather than truly listening to the other party. When you focus on your own response, you may miss critical information being communicated by the other party. This can lead to mistakes, misunderstandings, and inaccurate perspectives on the issues at hand.

> *"There is a difference between listening and waiting for your turn to speak."*
>
> — Simon Sinek

Additionally, if you appear visibly distracted or preoccupied with your own thoughts, the other party may perceive your behavior as disinterest or disrespect, which can damage trust. They may walk away feeling undervalued and disengaged from the discussion.

Focusing on your own response often hinders creative problem-solving. Effective solutions generally result from a deep understanding of all parties' perspectives and needs. Without fully listening, you may miss the opportunity to make informed decisions and effectively advocate for your position, which can weaken your negotiation stance.

Finally, not fully listening can even lead to escalating tensions and conflicts, as the other party may feel their concerns are not being acknowledged or addressed.

How to Stay Present and Engaged

First, strive to *"stay in the moment."* Mindfulness techniques can help you remain present and focused during negotiations. Pay attention to your thoughts and bring your focus back to the conversation if you find your mind wandering.

Second, make a conscious effort to engage fully with the speaker. This includes maintaining eye contact, nodding in acknowledgment, and providing verbal affirmations to show that you are listening. For example, Use phrases like *"I see," "That's interesting,"* or *"Tell me more"* to demonstrate that you are actively engaged with the discussion.

Next, as we've discussed in detail already, periodically reflect back and paraphrase what the other party has said to confirm your understanding and show that you are paying attention. For example: *"So, if I understand correctly, your main concern is . . . Is that right?"*

Remember to periodically summarize the discussion to ensure all parties are in agreement on the key points. For example, *"To summarize, we've agreed on . . . and will revisit . . . in our next meeting. Does that capture everything?"*

Finally, allow the speaker to finish their idea before responding. This demonstrates respect and ensures you fully understand their message.

IMPORTANT NINJA TIP: Mentally approach the negotiation with a desire to learn more about the other party's perspective. This attitude promotes mutual understanding. For instance, before preparing counterarguments, focus on understanding why the other party holds their views and how you can address their concerns.

Focusing on active listening and remaining mentally and emotionally present during negotiations can enhance communication and build stronger relationships. Moreover, avoiding the pitfall of focusing too much on your own response ensures that you fully understand the other party's perspective, leading to better problem-solving and collaboration.

Key Takeaways

Active listening is a fundamental skill that significantly enhances the negotiation process and the end result. It builds trust and creates an environment of mutual respect. When parties have open dialogue, the negotiation process is more transparent and productive, which in turn contributes to long-term, positive business relationships.

As a ninja negotiator, it is critically important to accurately understand the other party's true needs. This allows you to prioritize their objectives and adjust your proposal accordingly. Listening carefully also helps reveal the deeper interests and motivations behind the other party's stated positions.

Finally, clarifying assumptions through paraphrasing and allowing the speaker to finish their thoughts ensures complete understanding and shows respect. This builds trust throughout the negotiating process and allows for proactive problem-solving and conflict prevention.

In summary, listening more than you speak is essential for successful negotiations. It builds trust, uncovers deeper insights, improves problem-solving, and prevents common pitfalls. Structured goal-setting enhances these benefits by providing clear objectives and ensuring effective communication and decision-making.

In the next chapter, we'll tackle the difficult challenge of knowing when to walk away from the negotiating table.

CHAPTER 5
Be Ready to Walk Away

"If you know the enemy and know yourself you need not fear the results of a hundred battles."
— Sun Tzu

As a ninja negotiator, you will inevitably face a fundamental truth:

Not all deals are worth pursuing.

Or, in the words of my best friend, "*Sometimes, the juice just ain't worth the squeeze.*"

So, why do amateur negotiators accept bad deals?

One of our most natural fears is loss, commonly referred to as the "*fear of missing out*" (i.e., FOMO). This fear commonly arises during negotiations. You might fear walking away from the negotiating table, thinking that it automatically signals failure or a missed opportunity of a lifetime.

This fear commonly stems from pressure to secure deals, build partnerships, or support the growth of your business. However, it can also lead you to accept unfavorable terms that may undermine your business in the long run. A willingness to walk away is not a sign of weakness but a testament to your clarity about your business goals, values, and self-worth. This ensures that you only enter into deals that align with your business objectives and protect your interests.

Being prepared to walk away forces you to clearly define your top priorities. This ensures that you remain focused on achieving your goals and don't get sidetracked by less important issues. Having the strength to walk away enhances your negotiation power by providing leverage. It shows that you have viable alternatives and are not dependent on a single supplier or client, which encourages the other party to make concessions.

Demonstrating a willingness to walk away also builds respect and credibility. It signals to the other party that you are serious about your terms and committed to achieving a fair but mutually beneficial deal. It promotes balanced agreements where both sides feel satisfied with the terms.

REMEMBER: *Being willing to walk away is not a sign of weakness but a testament to your clarity about your business goals, values, and self-worth.*

As a negotiation ninja, you will make more strategic, confident, and fair decisions by being prepared to walk away. This principle not only enhances negotiation results but also builds stronger and more respectful relationships with the other party.

Know When to Leave the Table

Knowing when to leave the negotiating table can be tricky. On the one hand, you don't want to miss a great opportunity. On the other hand, you don't want to waste time or continue a negotiation that has become stagnant or has no real possibility of moving forward or satisfying your core objectives.

To determine the right time to walk away, you must identify your non-negotiable points and negotiate in good faith without compromising your core values.

Let's examine each of these in more detail.

How to Define Non-Negotiables

Understanding your non-negotiables is critical when negotiating. It ensures that you don't compromise on essential terms that could harm your long-term interests. Non-negotiables are the boundaries that you must maintain for the agreement to be acceptable.

To start, you have to know what's most important to you. Core values are what guide your decisions and actions. In a negotiation, these values help you determine which terms are absolutely essential and, therefore, non-negotiable.

Consider the long-term impact of each term. If agreeing to a term could have negative (or severe) consequences on your business or personal goals, it is probably non-negotiable.

IMPORTANT NINJA TIP: If you're negotiating on behalf of a third party, corporation, or entity, it is important to engage with key stakeholders, such as team members, advisors, partners, or corporate attorneys, to identify non-negotiables. This collective input ensures that all critical perspectives are considered.

Once you have your objectives clearly in mind, rank them based on their importance. High-priority objectives are likely to be non-negotiable, while lower-priority objectives may offer some room for compromise. Clearly identify deal breakers—terms that, if not met, would lead you to walk away from the negotiation. These deal breakers define your bottom line.

Understanding your non-negotiables allows you to approach negotiations with clarity and confidence. This ensures that you protect your essential interests and make informed decisions about when to walk away. Recognizing your absolute limits and maintaining a firm stance on non-negotiable terms sharpens your negotiating prowess.

Read the Room

When determining the ideal moment to walk away from a negotiation, it is also crucial to assess the situation thoroughly. This involves analyzing the progress of the negotiation, recognizing signs of a deadlock, and understanding the overall dynamics at play. By evaluating these factors, you can make informed decisions about whether to continue negotiating or to leave.

Signs of a Deadlock

Here are some signs to look for:

Stagnant Discussions. If the same arguments and points are repeated without any forward movement, the negotiation may be at a deadlock.

No Flexibility. When neither party is willing to make concessions or consider alternative solutions, the negotiation is likely stalled.

Breakdown in Dialogue. A significant reduction in communication, such as delayed responses or avoidance of key issues, can signal that the negotiation is not progressing.

Increased Tension / Escalating Conflict. Rising tension and escalating conflict are strong indicators of a deadlock. If emotions are running high and disputes are becoming more frequent, the negotiation may be stuck.

Unchanged Offers or Proposals. If offers and counteroffers remain unchanged over multiple rounds of negotiation, it indicates that neither party is willing to budge. Likewise, if minor issues are taking an inordinate amount of time to resolve, it suggests that larger, more complex issues will likely remain unresolved.

Gut Feeling / Intuition. Sometimes, a gut feeling that the negotiation is going nowhere can be a valuable indicator. Trusting your intuition, especially if it is based on experience, can guide you in recognizing a deadlock.

By analyzing the progress of the negotiation and recognizing signs of a deadlock, you can make informed decisions about whether to continue negotiating or to walk away. This strategic assessment helps you avoid wasting time and resources on unproductive discussions and focus on pursuing more viable alternatives.

Don't Compromise Core Values

During negotiations, it is important to clearly communicate your core values and why they are non-negotiable. This transparency helps the other party understand your priorities and reduces misunderstandings. For example: *"Our commitment to . . . means we cannot compromise on . . . "*

Whenever possible, frame your firm stance in a positive light, emphasizing the benefits of adhering to your core values for both parties. For example: *"Maintaining these high-quality standards ensures that we deliver a reliable product that meets your customers' expectations and enhances your brand reputation."* Also, emphasize the long-term benefits of adhering to your core values, showing how these values contribute to long-term success and mutual benefits.

Finally, when standing firm on core values, seek creative alternatives that address the other party's concerns without compromising your principles. For instance, If you cannot lower your product price, offer added value through enhanced support or other services.

By balancing firmness with adaptability and finding ways to negotiate without compromising core values, you can achieve favorable results while maintaining your principles. This approach ensures that you protect your essential interests and build strong, sustainable agreements that align with your long-term goals.

Manage Your Emotions and Maintain Professionalism

Okay. Let's be frank. There are times when negotiating feels like mental and emotional warfare.

That's because it is.

The key to walking away with a sense of inner peace lies in mental and emotional preparation, learning to recognize and manage emotional triggers, and avoiding common pressure tactics designed to make you compromise or make unreasonable concessions.

Let's start with mental preparation.

Prepare Mentally and Emotionally

Preparing mentally and emotionally for the possibility of walking away from a negotiation is essential for maintaining confidence, calmness, and resilience throughout the process.

Start by visualizing a successful negotiation. This mental rehearsal helps you approach the negotiation with a positive mindset.

Next, be sure to do your homework. As we discussed in a prior chapter, thorough preparation is key to feeling confident. Know your facts, understand the other party's position, and be clear about your own goals and limits.

Finally, set realistic expectations regarding the outcome of the negotiation process. Understand that not every negotiation will result in an agreement. Setting realistic expectations helps you stay calm and focused on your goals without feeling undue pressure to compromise in order to reach an agreement quickly.

REMEMBER: *You must accept that walking away is a valid outcome if the terms do not meet your minimum requirements.*

Avoid Pressure Tactics

To begin with, remember that all negotiations involve competing interests. When one side feels like they are not getting the desired results, pressure tactics are sometimes used to gain leverage. By recognizing pressure tactics like ultimatums or time constraints, you can prepare strategies to handle them without feeling rushed or coerced.

Emotional triggers, in addition to ultimatums, are sometimes used. Learning to identify these triggers allows you to manage your responses more effectively. When you feel frustration building, take a brief pause before responding. This brief moment of clarity allows you to collect your thoughts and respond more thoughtfully.

In addition, use *"I"* statements to express your feelings constructively without blaming or accusing the other party. For example: *"I feel concerned about . . . because it may impact our ability to deliver . . ."* Rather than resort to personal attacks or arguments, keep the discussion focused on the issue at hand.

Active listening can also help defuse tension and show that you respect the other party's perspective, even if you disagree. For example: *"I understand that you have concerns about . . . Let's explore how we can address those concerns within our constraints."*

Don't be afraid to stand your ground — clearly communicate and maintain your boundaries, even in the face of pressure. Standing firm on your limits demonstrates confidence and resolve. For example: *"I understand your urgency, but we need to ensure that the terms also align with our strategic goals before proceeding."*

Finally, take a moment to pause the negotiation if emotions are running high. This will allow everyone to cool down and return with a clearer perspective. For example, you might say: *"Let's take a 10-minute break to gather our thoughts and come back to this discussion with fresh perspectives."*

By preparing mentally and emotionally for the possibility of walking away, you enhance your ability to navigate the negotiation process with confidence and composure. These techniques help you manage stress, maintain professionalism, and avoid succumbing to pressure tactics, ensuring that you make smart, informed decisions that align with your goals.

Leave the Table on Good Terms

There are times when walking away from the negotiating table is just the sensible thing to do. However, it is always wise to leave the table without "burning bridges" with the other party, if at all possible.

Leaving on good terms shows that you are thinking strategically instead of allowing emotions to sabotage any hope of future bargaining. When both parties feel respected, even without an agreement, the possibility is left open for future discussions.

REMEMBER: *Winning does not always mean that the negotiation is successful. Sometimes, the other party is unwilling to pay what is fair or meet reasonable demands. Ending on a positive note minimizes conflict and prevents negative fallout, reducing the risk of lingering resentment or hostility.*

Additionally, maintaining professionalism and ethical standards throughout the negotiating process preserves your dignity and self-respect. Handling difficult negotiations with grace reinforces your personal and professional values.

Despite the tone and direction of the negotiation, demonstrating professionalism positively reflects your respect, integrity, and ethical behavior. This commitment reinforces your commitment to ethical practices.

Maintaining respect and courtesy regardless of the outcome of the negotiation ensures that you leave the table on good terms, enhances your professional reputation, and preserves relationships, keeping the possibility open for future opportunities.

Common Pitfalls to Avoid

When it comes to being prepared to walk away from the negotiating table, there are 3 common pitfalls that should be avoided. The inherent fear of walking away, negotiating past your walking away point, and not having an alternative strategy.

Let's start with the fear of walking away.

Fear of Walking Away

Parties with stronger bargaining power commonly exploit the fear of walking away. The thought of missing out on a *"once-in-a-lifetime"* opportunity leads the other party into the trap of accepting unfavorable terms that compromise their long-term objectives. Overcoming this fear is crucial for maintaining a strong negotiation position and achieving a favorable outcome.

To start, weigh the consequences of both walking away and accepting terms that fail to meet your requirements. Compare the potential short-term gains of accepting a deal with the long-term costs of compromising on critical terms.

Next, know your clear walk-away points before entering negotiations. This reduces the chance of making hasty compromises out of fear.

Additionally, reframe the mindset around walking away. View it as a strategic decision that protects your interests rather than as a failure or loss. Consider walking away as a positive step towards finding a better opportunity that aligns with your goals and values.

By evaluating the consequences, focusing on core values, reframing your mindset, and knowing your walk-away points, you can maintain a strong negotiation position and avoid unfavorable compromises.

Negotiating Past Your Walk-Away Point

Negotiating beyond your pre-determined walk-away point is another critical mistake that can lead to unfavorable agreements that undermine your long-term goals. Staying true to your boundaries is essential for maintaining a strong negotiation position.

As negotiations progress, we sometimes fail to take a step back and remember the minimum acceptable criteria. The excitement of the moment can overshadow the boundaries we set for negotiation. However, ignoring your walk-away point can result in agreements misaligned with your long-term goals. This can have lasting negative impacts on your overall objectives.

To prevent this, briefly review your walk-away points before entering negotiations. Make sure that they are realistic, achievable, and aligned with your overall goals. Likewise, regularly review and reaffirm your non-negotiable terms throughout the negotiating process to stay focused and committed. Especially during long-term negotiations, periodically reassess your boundaries to ensure the discussion remains relevant and on par with your objectives.

Remove emotion from the equation by basing your walk-away points on objective criteria such as market rates, industry standards, and financial analysis. This strengthens your position and provides a rational basis for the boundaries you set.

Anticipate potential objections and challenges from the other party and prepare to respond in a way that supports your boundaries. Communicate using assertive yet respectful language to clearly convey your walk-away points and their rationale.

Finally, mentally visualize the positive outcomes of adhering to your walk-away points and the potential negative consequences of compromising them. This mental preparation helps reinforce your boundaries. Imagine the satisfaction of securing a deal that aligns with your goals and the regret of accepting terms that undermine your interests.

By understanding the risks of compromising on your walk-away points and using strategies to stay true to your boundaries, you can protect your interests and secure a more favorable negotiation. This commitment enhances your credibility, strengthens your negotiation position, and ensures that agreements align with your long-term goals and values.

Failing to Prepare Alternatives

The third pitfall in walking away is failing to prepare strong alternatives. Without a well-defined BATNA (Best Alternative to a Negotiated Agreement), you lack leverage, confidence, and options if negotiations fail.

Without a BATNA, you will be tempted to rely heavily on reaching an agreement, which weakens your position and makes you more susceptible to unfavorable terms. Moreover, there is increased vulnerability to pressure tactics and demands, leading to compromises on critical issues.

REMEMBER: *Decisions made from fear of losing a deal generally result in agreements that are not in your best interest. Accepting unfavorable terms can harm your reputation, making you seem weak or desperate in future negotiations.*

To avoid this, periodically research the market to identify potential alternatives, including vendors, partners, or suppliers. Keep a list of both preferred and alternatives for each.

Actively network and build relationships within your industry to identify additional opportunities. Having a strong network provides valuable alternatives.

Finally, review and update your BATNA regularly to reflect changes in the market and your goals. Create backup strategies for different scenarios, providing clear alternatives if the primary negotiation fails.

By preparing and maintaining a strong BATNA, you enhance your negotiation power and confidence and increase the likelihood of securing a favorable negotiation result. Having alternatives ensures that you never feel pressured into accepting unfavorable terms and allows you to negotiate from a position of strength and flexibility.

Key Takeaways

In this chapter, we emphasized the importance of being prepared to walk away from negotiations and the various elements that support this approach. Defining clear walk-away points helps maintain firm stances and avoid compromising on critical issues, ensuring alignment with your goals and values.

Balancing firmness with flexibility on less critical terms can facilitate agreement and build goodwill. Likewise, emotional control and professionalism are vital for clear thinking and effective communication. Recognizing and avoiding common pitfalls, such as the fear of walking away, ignoring your walk-away points, and failing to prepare alternatives, ensures a better outcome.

Strong alternatives and setting clear boundaries also enhance negotiation power by providing leverage. They improve decision-making by ensuring rational choices and protect interests by adhering to walk-away points that align with long-term objectives and values. Maintaining these boundaries consistently builds your credibility and a reputation for integrity.

Thorough preparation ensures you enter negotiations with a solid plan. Staying true to your core values and non-negotiables is crucial for maintaining integrity and managing stress, allowing for more confident and assertive discussions.

In the next chapter, we'll discuss the mechanics of creating strategic offers and counteroffers.

CHAPTER 6
Mastering Offers and Counteroffers

"Successful negotiation is not about getting to 'yes'; it's about mastering 'no' and understanding what the path to an agreement is."
– Christopher Voss

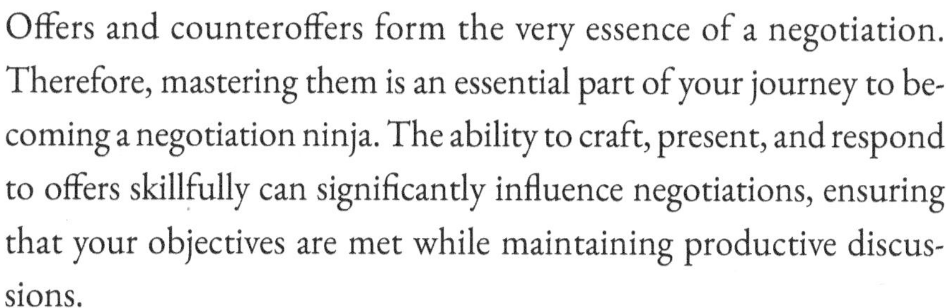

Offers and counteroffers form the very essence of a negotiation. Therefore, mastering them is an essential part of your journey to becoming a negotiation ninja. The ability to craft, present, and respond to offers skillfully can significantly influence negotiations, ensuring that your objectives are met while maintaining productive discussions.

Strategic offers and counteroffers set the negotiation tone and create a well-defined starting point. A strong initial offer can serve as an anchor, shaping perceptions and steering the negotiation in your favor. Responding strategically with counteroffers shows assertiveness and flexibility, creating a collaborative atmosphere and building trust.

Remember, the ultimate goal of any offer is to provide mutual benefit and walk away with a sustainable agreement. By carefully crafting and presenting your offer, you can keep the negotiation process flowing in a positive direction.

A strong initial offer serves as a foundation for negotiation. It sets the tone for the negotiation and establishes a clear starting point. It communicates your position and intentions, providing a framework for the discussion.

Let's see how to create the initial offer.

How to Craft Your Initial Offer

Creating a strong initial offer sets the tone for the discussion — establishing a baseline for further negotiations. Your initial offer has an *"anchoring effect."* It influences the perceptions of the other party from the start — guiding how subsequent offers and counteroffers are perceived. Thus, a well-crafted offer can steer the negotiation in your favor.

Here are the steps to crafting a solid initial offer:

1. ***Conduct Thorough Research.*** Understand market conditions, industry standards, and the other party's needs and constraints to craft a realistic and competitive offer.

2. ***Be Specific and Detailed.*** Provide specific details about terms, conditions, and justifications to reduce ambiguity and prompt thoughtful consideration.

3. ***Highlight Value and Benefits.*** Clearly express the value and benefits of your offer, making it more attractive by em-

phasizing how it meets the other party's needs and solves their pain points.

4. ***Use Positive Framing.*** Frame the initial offer in a way that focuses on mutual benefits and how the offer aligns with the other party's long-term goals.

5. ***Be Realistic.*** Ensure the offer is achievable and within realistic bounds to maintain credibility and avoid stalling negotiations.

6. ***Anticipate Counteroffers.*** Prepare responses to possible counteroffers to maintain the integrity of your initial offer while showing a willingness to negotiate.

Crafting a strong initial offer lays a solid foundation for the negotiation process, builds credibility, and creates momentum toward a mutually beneficial agreement.

When to Present Your Offer

Knowing when to present your offer is another crucial step in the negotiation process. Presenting your offer at the right moment will increase the likelihood of acceptance.

To do this, start by assessing the overall context of the negotiation, including the other party's readiness and mood. Both parties should be in a suitable frame of mind to move forward. Be sure to allow enough time for information to be exchanged before making your offer. Ensure that you have gathered enough insights into the other party's needs, constraints, and priorities.

As the discussions continue, pay attention to verbal and nonverbal cues that indicate the other party's readiness to receive your offer. Signals such as open body language, positive responses, and engagement suggest the right moment.

By carefully considering the timing of your offer, you can enhance its impact and increase the likelihood of a positive response. Effective timing demonstrates strategic thinking, respects the negotiation process, and aligns with the other party's readiness and priorities.

How to Frame the Offer Correctly

Have you ever noticed that upscale art galleries go to great lengths to expertly matte and frame valuable works of art?

Do you know why?

Well, even though the piece of art may look like the work of a deranged third grader, the way it's framed and presented to the public gives it credibility and makes it much more attractive. The mere act of framing the art correctly provides a backdrop and context and enhances its overall appeal. Thus, the gallery can charge a premium to a potential buyer.

In a similar context, framing your offer correctly is a critical element of successful negotiation. This ensures that the offer is positively received, clearly understood, and more attractive to the other party. The presentation of your offer significantly influences the likelihood of acceptance and supports the momentum of the negotiation. Frame your offer by using persuasive language, avoiding vague or overly complex terms that might confuse the other party.

Focusing on the other party's needs and interests is also crucial to making your offer appealing. Tailor your proposal to address the other party's specific pain points, demonstrating an intimate understanding of their needs and how your offer can meet them. This approach makes your offer more attractive. For example, *"We know . . . is a priority for your company. Our solution meets this need by . . ."*

Similarly, it is vital to remember that everyone loves a good story.

Why?

Authentic stories inspire and resonate with us on the deepest emotional levels. Therefore, include storytelling techniques to make your offer more engaging and relatable, sharing success stories or case studies from other clients that demonstrate the benefits of your offer.

When framing your offer, do your best to anticipate potential objections and address them proactively, showing that you understand the other party's concerns and have already considered solutions. Be sure to emphasize any unique features or benefits that provide the other party added value.

Finally, quantify the benefits of your offer with concrete numbers and data to add credibility. Providing specific facts and figures helps the other party see the tangible value of your proposal, making it easier for them to justify acceptance. Highlight the long-term value of your offer, not just immediate gains.

By framing your offer effectively, you enhance its appeal and increase the likelihood of a positive response. Using persuasive language, clear communication, and emphasizing the benefits and value of your offer are key strategies for a successful negotiation.

Okay, let's pivot and take a look at how to make effective counteroffers.

How to Make Counteroffers

Knowing how to make an effective counteroffer is another essential piece of the negotiation process. This demonstrates your ability to engage strategically with the other party's proposal.

Start by critically evaluating the initial offer presented to you. Thoroughly consider its terms, conditions, and underlying assumptions to fully comprehend what is being proposed. Carefully weigh the benefits and drawbacks of the initial offer to determine which aspects are acceptable and which ones warrant further discussion.

Additionally, consider the broader context of the negotiation, including market conditions, industry standards, and the other party's position, to gain valuable insight into the motivations behind the offer. Anticipate how the other party might react, preparing for further negotiation and adjusting your strategy accordingly.

During the negotiation, start your counteroffer by acknowledging the positive aspects of the initial offer. This approach shows appreciation for their proposal and sets a collaborative tone. Next, clearly address the key issues that need improvement or adjustment. Be specific about what changes you are requesting and why they are important. Support your counteroffer with rational arguments and data to make your request more persuasive and reasonable.

Be sure to indicate areas where you are willing to be flexible. Be prepared to make concessions in areas that are less critical to you.

Offering concessions can facilitate agreement and demonstrate good faith. For example: *"We are open to discussing . . . in exchange for . . ."*

Finally, summarize your counteroffer clearly, ensuring that all points are understood and agreed upon. Confirming details helps prevent misunderstandings when finalizing the deal.

By critically assessing the initial offer and responding with a strategic counteroffer, you can work towards a mutually beneficial agreement. These techniques help you address key issues, support your requests with rational arguments, and maintain a positive and collaborative negotiation atmosphere.

Negotiation Tactics to Avoid

As you continue to hone your negotiating skills toward becoming a negotiation ninja, some tactics should be avoided. Namely, lowballing or highballing the other party and using hardball tactics to force the other party to compromise.

Let's start with lowballing and highballing.

Lowballing and Highballing

Lowballing and highballing are common negotiation tactics. While some non-ninjas may use these strategies to set the stage for negotiations, they carry significant risks and potential consequences.

Lowball and highball offers damage relationships by eroding trust. If the other party perceives the offer as unreasonable or insincere, it can make negotiations more difficult. This can also lead to deadlocks, wasting time and resources. Negative perceptions often result because the other party views the offer as a sign of bad faith or a lack of seriousness, damaging credibility.

Often, lowballing and highballing tactics stem from a lack of respect for the other party or being ignorant of the true market value of the products and services being discussed. The effect is an immediate negative emotional reaction, such as frustration or anger, which escalates tensions and makes productive negotiations more challenging. In the mind of the other party, it is a clear indication of ignorance or disrespect — not good for productive negotiation.

To avoid making these amateur mistakes, start by doing your homework. You'll want to understand market conditions and the going rates for products and services. This information helps you make realistic, well-informed offers.

Instead of making disproportionate offers or counteroffers, use incremental adjustments to move closer to an agreement. This approach allows for more flexibility and adaptation during negotiations. Demonstrate your willingness to find common ground. This openness can encourage the other party to engage more constructively and collaboratively.

When negotiating, keep the long-term relationship in mind. Focus on building a foundation for future collaboration by maintaining positive momentum. It may help to put yourself in the other party's shoes when considering their needs, constraints, and motivations. Crafting an offer with empathy will lead to more productive and respectful negotiations.

Focusing on realistic, well-researched proposals will enhance the tone and pace of the negotiations. These strategies also help maintain credibility, trust and create a positive atmosphere.

Hardball Tactics

Hardball tactics are aggressive negotiation strategies designed to intimidate or pressure the other party into conceding. These are common among lawyers, larger corporations and situations where one party has a significant advantage over the other. While these tactics can sometimes yield short-term gains, most often they damage relationships and create long-term negative consequences.

Common hardball tactics include *"Stonewalling"* (or refusing to budge on any issue), such as stating: *"This is our final offer. Take it or leave it."* This makes it very difficult for the negotiation to progress, especially when one party rejects all proposals without providing reasons or alternatives.

"Bluffing" (or pretending to have more leverage than actually exists) is another common but risky tactic for coercing others. Similarly, the *"good cop, bad cop"* strategy is sometimes used — where one negotiator is harsh, and another is accommodating, alternating between confusion and pressure toward the other party.

Unfortunately, some negotiators even resort to direct intimidation tactics, including threats, aggressive behavior, or implied consequences, to force an agreement (like a supplier threatening to cease all future business unless their terms are accepted immediately).

Hardball tactics erode trust and harm relationships, making future negotiations extremely difficult. Potential long-term business partners will not want to do business when they feel bullied into an agreement. Additionally, using hardball tactics can harm your reputation in the industry, making others less likely to want to negotiate with you in the future. A person known for bluffing may find it much harder to establish relationships with new clients or partners.

REMEMBER: *Always negotiate in good faith. Avoid deceptive practices which involve misleading or intentionally providing false information to gain an advantage. While these tactics may seem to offer short-term benefits, they generally lead to long-term negative consequences, including potential lawsuits, penalties, and loss of licenses or certifications.*

How to Respond to Hardball Tactics

When faced with hardball tactics from the other party, it is easy to feel intimidated and pressured to back down immediately. However, here are some strategies that will help you respond appropriately:

Stay Calm and Composed. Maintain your composure and avoid reacting emotionally to aggressive tactics. This helps you think clearly and respond effectively.

Call Out the Behavior. Politely but firmly call out aggressive tactics and express your desire for a more collaborative approach. For example: *"I notice that this offer is presented as non-negotiable. Can we explore some options that might work better for both of us?"*

Ask Clarifying Questions. Ask clarifying questions to understand the rationale behind the aggressive stance. This can help defuse the situation and bring the focus back to constructive dialogue. For example: *"Can you help me understand why this term is so important to you?"*

Deflect Aggression. Use neutral and non-confrontational language to deflect aggression and steer the conversation towards problem-solving. For example: *"Let's take a step back and look at the bigger picture to find a solution that meets both our needs."*

Shift the Focus by Reframing. Reframe the discussion to focus on mutual goals and interests rather than positions. This approach can help de-escalate tension and promote collaboration. For example: *"Our goal is to achieve a successful partnership. How can we adjust these terms to benefit both sides?"*

Stand Your Ground on Core Issues. While it's important to be flexible, remain firm on your core issues and non-negotiables. Demonstrating resolve can discourage further use of hardball tactics. For example: *"We cannot compromise on . . . due to . . . , but we are open to discussing other aspects of the agreement."*

By identifying hardball tactics and knowing how to respond when faced with them, you can maintain a productive and respectful negotiation environment. These strategies help protect your interests, build trust, and preserve long-term positive relationships.

Common Pitfalls to Avoid

When making offers and counteroffers, there are a few common pitfalls that you should certainly avoid if you want to ensure a successful negotiation: lack of insight and empathy, rushing the negotiation process, and being inflexible and unwilling to compromise.

Let's take a closer look at each of these.

Lack of Insight and Empathy

When negotiating, it is crucial to consider the other party's perspective. Overlooking their needs, concerns, and motivations can lead to misunderstandings, conflicts, and, ultimately, a failed negotiation. Demonstrating an understanding of the other party's perspective also shows that you value their input and are committed to finding a solution that works for both sides.

Considering the other party's needs encourages open and honest communication, leading to a more transparent negotiation process where both parties feel heard and respected. This makes finding common ground easier, as it helps you both identify shared goals. Commonality often serves as the basis for finding an agreement that satisfies both parties.

To demonstrate insight and empathy for the other party, start by using active listening techniques to truly understand the other party's perspective. This involves paying attention, asking clarifying questions, and reflecting on their needs and concerns.

Acknowledge the other party's challenges and demonstrate a willingness to address them. For example: *"I understand that your budget is tight this quarter. Let's explore ways we can adjust the payment terms to fit your financial constraints."*

Additionally, negotiations should be approached as a collaborative problem-solving exercise rather than a zero-sum game. Focus on solutions that address both parties' needs. For example: *"How can we structure this agreement to ensure we both benefit and achieve our respective goals?"*

Finally, periodically check in with the other party and seek confirmation during the negotiation process. This helps ensure that their needs are being addressed and allows for adjustments as necessary. For example, *"Is there anything in our current proposal that doesn't meet your expectations? Let's work together to address any concerns."*

By actively considering the other party's perspective, you can facilitate open communication and work toward a mutually beneficial solution. These strategies also help prevent conflicts and lead to more sustainable agreements.

Rushing the Process

Another common pitfall is rushing the process when making offers and counteroffers. This often leads to overlooked details and poor decisions. Taking the time to thoroughly evaluate and discuss each term of the negotiation is essential for successful negotiations.

When the negotiation process is rushed, critical information, such as specific terms, conditions, or potential issues that could impact the agreement's success, might be missed. Incomplete or poorly structured agreements lack clear definitions and terms, possibly leading to disputes and misunderstandings later.

Inadequate risk assessment can become another significant problem when negotiations are hurried. Without a thorough risk assessment, you might overlook potential challenges or issues. This often leads to poor decisions, which also results from hasty negotiations. Impulsive offers that are not fully thought through can lead to agreements that don't address your needs or protect your interests and might even expose you to legal risks.

Finally, you can undermine your negotiation power when you appear rushed. The other party might perceive you as desperate or overly eager to close the deal, which can lead to being offered a less favorable deal.

To avoid this, start by preparing thoroughly before each negotiation session. Research relevant data, identify key negotiating points, and anticipate potential challenges. Be sure to set realistic timelines for the negotiation process to ensure that all aspects are thoroughly considered without unnecessary time pressure.

Throughout the negotiation process, take a step-by-step approach. Break down the negotiation process into manageable steps, allowing for focused and detailed discussions on each element. Always remember to stay calm, even if the negotiation process takes longer than expected. Rushing can lead to mistakes, while patience can lead to better outcomes.

Patience and thoroughness can make you more effective. This helps ensure that all details are considered, decisions are well-informed, and agreements are sustainable.

Being Inflexible

The third common pitfall when making offers and counteroffers concerns flexibility. A rigid approach hinders progress and alienates the other party. This often leads to increased conflict and tension, making it difficult to reach an agreement and potentially escalating disputes.

Inflexibility by one or both parties can cause negotiations to stall or reach a deadlock, where neither party is willing to make concessions, preventing any progress toward a mutually beneficial agreement.

Ultimately, remember that no one wants to walk away from the table feeling empty-handed or as though they were taken advantage of. Embracing a more open and collaborative approach helps build stronger relationships, find innovative solutions, and reach agreements that satisfy all parties.

In order to keep negotiations moving forward, start by knowing your boundaries. Clearly distinguish between your non-negotiable terms and areas where you can be more flexible. This understanding helps you focus on what truly matters while being open to compromise on other points.

Actively listen to fully understand the other party's needs, concerns, and motivations. This helps you pinpoint areas where flexibility can lead to a mutually beneficial solution. Keep an open mind and avoid making assumptions about the other party's intentions or limitations. Being open to new ideas and fresh perspectives leads to innovative solutions.

Also, remember to be strategic while maintaining an open mind. Making conditional concessions while still protecting your core interests encourages the other party to reciprocate. For example, *"We can agree to . . . if you can commit to . . . "*

Think in terms of long-term benefits, such as building stronger relationships and creating sustainable agreements. Long-term thinking often helps justify short-term compromises.

Finally, periodically reassess your position and be willing to adjust your negotiation stance based on new information or changes in circumstances. Flexibility requires ongoing evaluation and adaptation. For instance, during negotiations, be open to adjusting terms if new regulatory changes, market fluctuations, or supply chain challenges impact the feasibility of the original agreement.

Maintaining adaptability and openness helps prevent conflicts, builds stronger relationships, and leads to mutually beneficial agreements that are more likely to be honored and sustained over time.

Key Takeaways

In this chapter, we've discussed the fundamentals of mastering offers and counteroffers, understanding the importance of empathy, and crafting realistic proposals. You've also seen some of the hardball tactics that should be avoided, recognizing their potential for short-term gains but ultimately damaging long-term relationships.

We've explored how to respond effectively to these aggressive strategies, maintaining your composure and calling out the behavior while asking clarifying questions. At the same time, you've seen the importance of negotiating in good faith, avoiding deceptive practices, recognizing the risks, and maintaining integrity and trust.

Overall, you now have a comprehensive understanding of effective negotiation tactics and strategies, equipping yourself with the knowledge to build strong, sustainable relationships that lead to long-term success.

Hopefully, by this point, you're gaining more confidence in your ability to secure a favorable deal. Yes, you're nearing the end of your journey to becoming a negotiation ninja.

Let's move on to mastering the art of gaining leverage and making concessions.

CHAPTER 7
The Art of Leverage and Concessions

"Everything is a negotiation. Everything is a little bit of give and take."

— Lamman Rucker

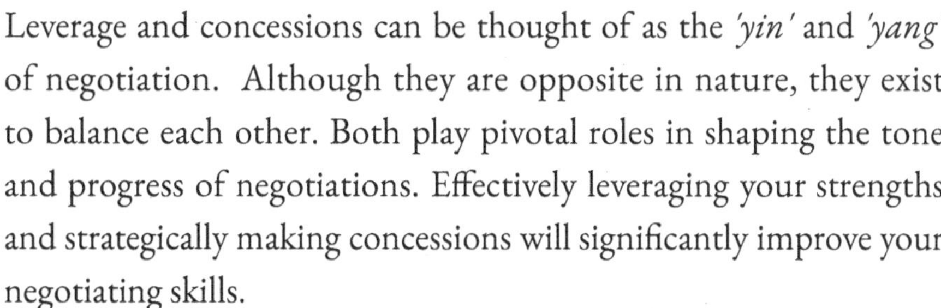

Leverage and concessions can be thought of as the *'yin'* and *'yang'* of negotiation. Although they are opposite in nature, they exist to balance each other. Both play pivotal roles in shaping the tone and progress of negotiations. Effectively leveraging your strengths and strategically making concessions will significantly improve your negotiating skills.

Let's start by understanding leverage.

What Exactly is Leverage?

Leverage refers to the advantages or strengths you (or the party that you represent) possess that can be used to influence the other party and steer the negotiation in your favor. It refers to any power (real or perceived) that one party has over another in negotiations.

What you bring to the table can really influence the other party's decisions and actions. Skillfully wielding influence allows you to assert your position more strongly and negotiate terms that are more favorable.

The 4 Types of Leverage

Leverage can be positive, negative, normative, or personal. All can be highly effective during negotiations.

1. ***Positive leverage*** is based on something the other party wants or needs. This could be a highly valued product, service, relationship, or opportunity.

2. ***Negative leverage*** is based on the ability to impose costs or consequences on the other party. This might include the power to enforce penalties, withdraw from a deal, or create adverse outcomes for the other party.

3. ***Normative leverage*** is based on standards, norms, or principles that the other party values or has agreed to (or is mandated by law). This type of leverage appeals to fairness, judicial precedent, compliance, or ethical standards.

4. ***Personal leverage*** stems from personal relationships, reputation, or influence. It is the power that comes from who you are, who you know (personally or professionally), and how you are perceived by others.

How to Gain Leverage

Gaining leverage will help you before and throughout the negotiation process. This involves building on your existing strengths and positioning yourself to maximize your influence.

Here are some ways to accomplish this:

Offer Something Unique. Continuously innovate and develop unique products or services that set you apart from competitors. Unique products and services can significantly enhance your leverage by providing something the other party cannot easily find elsewhere.

Have a Strong Financial Position. Maintain a strong financial portfolio. Financial stability allows you to negotiate from a position of strength and resist pressure to make unfavorable concessions.

Expand Market Reach. Work on increasing your market share within your specific niche or industry. A broad market presence enhances your leverage by demonstrating your influence and reach.

Build Partnerships and Alliances. Build and nurture strategic partnerships and alliances that enhance your position. Relationships with influential partners can provide additional leverage points.

Invest in Brand Equity for Reputation and Trust. Invest in building a strong brand and reputation. A well-regarded brand enhances your leverage by building trust and making your offers more attractive.

Improve Efficiency. Streamline your operational efficiency to reduce costs and improve reliability. Operational strengths can be leveraged to negotiate better terms and conditions.

By implementing these strategies, you can significantly enhance your leverage in negotiations. More leverage allows you to negotiate more effectively and more robust agreements.

Using Information as Leverage

Having access to the right information is a powerful tool that can significantly enhance your leverage and influence the outcome. Comprehensive and accurate information enables you to make informed decisions, present compelling arguments, and anticipate the other party's moves.

Competitive Intelligence

Relatively few small business owners understand the value of competitive intelligence. Gathering competitive intelligence about your competitors' strengths, weaknesses, strategies, and market positioning can help you anticipate their moves and develop effective counterstrategies.

Start by analyzing competitors' strategies, strengths, and weaknesses through the lens of your own market research. This allows you to differentiate your proposal and highlight your unique advantages. If possible, analyze historical data by reviewing past records to identify patterns and trends. This information can provide valuable insights into what has worked well and what hasn't.

Know your stuff

When presenting intelligence data, always provide context for the data you present. Explain what the data means, why it is relevant, and how it supports your argument. Use storytelling techniques to weave data into a compelling narrative. This makes your proposal more engaging and memorable. Use comparative data to benchmark your position against industry standards or competitors. This helps the other party see how your offer stacks up in the broader market context.

Well-informed negotiators present more compelling arguments. Therefore, it is important to understand current and emerging market trends, shifts in demand, pricing, and competitive strategies. It is also wise to use this information to gain insights into customer preferences and behaviors. Tailor your negotiation strategy to align with what customers value most.

Keep up with regulatory and policy trends that could impact your negotiation. Use this information to anticipate challenges and position your proposal as compliant and forward-thinking. Additionally, economic indicators such as GDP growth, inflation rates, and consumer confidence indexes can provide a macroeconomic perspective. This helps contextualize your position within the broader economic environment.

Finally, don't forget to consider any geopolitical factors and global market trends that could influence your negotiation. Understanding these dynamics helps you anticipate risks and identify opportunities.

By leveraging market research and industry trends, you can strengthen your negotiation position and make more compelling arguments. Data-driven negotiations are more persuasive and credible, helping you create more favorable agreements.

Anticipate the Other Party's Moves

Once you have gathered enough information, it can be used to anticipate the other party's moves throughout the negotiation. This can give you a significant strategic advantage. By predicting their strategies and understanding their motivations, you can prepare effectively and position yourself to respond effectively.

Start by identifying the primary objectives and motivations of the other party. Knowing what they value most helps you predict their moves and prepare counterstrategies. For example: Recognizing that a client prioritizes cost savings over product features allows you to tailor your proposals accordingly.

Next, conduct a SWOT analysis (Strengths, Weaknesses, Opportunities, Threats) of the other party to better understand their position. This helps you predict their strategies based on their strengths and areas where they might be willing to concede. For example, Identifying financial instability as a weakness might make the other party more flexible on payment terms.

Also, keep track of market and industry trends that could influence the other party's strategies. External factors play a significant role in shaping negotiation tactics. For instance, a recent downturn in the industry (or other market dynamics) might make the other party more eager to close a deal quickly.

Based on what you've learned, develop counterstrategies that address the other party's likely moves. Being proactive rather than reactive gives you a strategic edge. For instance, If you anticipate that the other party will push for a lower price, prepare data to justify your pricing and highlight the additional value you offer.

Throughout the negotiation, use your knowledge to steer the negotiation in a direction that favors your objectives. You can guide the discussion toward your desired outcomes by anticipating the other party's moves.

You can significantly improve your position by predicting and preparing for the other party's strategies. Using this knowledge to your advantage allows you to develop effective counterstrategies, address their concerns, and steer the negotiation favorably.

Okay, let's move on to making concessions.

The Art of Making Concessions

Making strategic concessions is an integral part of negotiations. When used wisely, concessions help to break deadlocks and move negotiations forward. When parties reach an impasse, a well-timed concession can create momentum and encourage further discussion.

Overall, concessions foster a sense of reciprocity and goodwill. When one party makes a concession, it often encourages the other party to reciprocate, leading to a more balanced and cooperative negotiation process. This shows that you are flexible and willing to work towards a mutually acceptable solution, which builds trust and enhances the negotiating atmosphere.

Know When to Concede

Knowing when to concede is critical to the negotiating process, as it can significantly influence the outcome. Well-timed concessions can break stalemates, build momentum, and encourage reciprocal concessions from the other party. This involves basing concessions on the negotiation phase, reading signals, and conceding strategically.

Base Concessions on the Negotiation Phase

Initial Phase. Early in the negotiation, concessions should be minimal and used to set a positive tone. These initial concessions can help build goodwill and demonstrate your willingness to cooperate.

Middle Phase. As negotiations progress, concessions can become more substantial. This is the phase where both parties are likely to make significant moves to advance towards an agreement.

Final Phase. In the closing stages, concessions should be carefully calculated and mainly used to finalize the deal. Major concessions at this stage can help overcome final obstacles and seal the agreement.

Read the Other Party's Signals

Non-Verbal Cues. Pay attention to non-verbal cues such as body language, facial expressions, and tone of voice. These signals can indicate when the other party is receptive to concessions or when they are reaching their limits. For instance, Notice the other party's relieved body language when you mention a potential concession on pricing.

Verbal Signals. Listen for verbal hints that the other party is ready for a compromise. Phrases like *"What if we..."* or *"Could we consider..."* often indicate openness to negotiation and potential receptiveness to concessions.

By identifying the right moments to make concessions and using techniques to time them strategically, you can maximize their impact and enhance your negotiation outcomes. Well-timed concessions can facilitate progress, build goodwill, and create value for both parties.

How to Give In Without Feeling Taken

Balancing give and take is essential for equitable agreements in negotiations. Ensuring that both parties feel their interests are respected and valued produces a cooperative atmosphere and lays the foundation for a sustainable relationship.

Start by knowing the difference between major concessions that significantly impact your position and minor concessions that you can offer to build goodwill without compromising your core interests. Treat concessions as bargaining chips that you can use strategically to gain advantages in areas that are important to you.

Additionally, structure your concessions to create additional value for the other party while preserving your core interests. This approach ensures that concessions are seen as beneficial and not as compromises. Then, clearly communicate the benefits of your concessions to the other party. Emphasize how the concession meets their needs and adds value so that it is appreciated and reciprocated.

Furthermore, establish and maintain clear boundaries around your non-negotiable points. If necessary, communicate these boundaries to the other party to manage expectations.

Finally, always try to get *Quid Pro Quo* by making your concessions conditional on receiving something of equivalent value in return, which aligns with your core needs. This assures that concessions lead to reciprocal benefits and prevents one-sided agreements.

By effectively balancing give and take, you can ensure that concessions lead to mutually beneficial deals. Strategic concessions that do not compromise your core interests, combined with techniques for ensuring reciprocal concessions, create a solid foundation for successful negotiations.

Common Pitfalls to Avoid

When gaining leverage and making concessions, two major pitfalls must be avoided: over-conceding and misinterpreting the other party's concessions. Over-conceding can significantly weaken your position. Likewise, misunderstanding concessions can lead to confusion, misalignment, and, ultimately, the breakdown of negotiations.

Over-Conceding

Conceding too much erodes your leverage. Each unnecessary concession weakens your ability to influence the final agreement. Therefore, it's crucial to strike a balance between making concessions and protecting your core interests. Over-conceding also sets a negative precedent, leading the other party to expect similar concessions throughout the negotiation or in future negotiations.

Making too many concessions gives the other party the perception that you are weak and desperate. It may lead them to question your competence and look for more ways to undermine your negotiating position.

To avoid over-conceding, start by establishing and reinforcing your non-negotiable terms and limits. Sticking to these boundaries helps you resist pressure to concede. Similarly, focusing on your core interests allows you to make concessions on less critical issues while protecting your key priorities to maintain a balanced negotiating stance.

Concede incrementally rather than making large concessions upfront. This allows you to gauge the other party's response and maintain control over the negotiation process.

As you make concessions, ensure that the other party recognizes the value of your concessions. Emphasize how the concession meets their needs and supports their ultimate objectives, making it more likely to be appreciated and reciprocated.

Above all, stand your ground when necessary. Negotiate firmly and confidently. Resist the urge to make concessions in response to pressure tactics. Maintain your position on key issues to protect your interests.

You can protect your interests by avoiding over-conceding and using strategies to maintain a balanced and fair negotiation process. Setting clear boundaries, prioritizing core interests, and making conditional concessions ensures that your negotiation approach is effective and sustainable.

Misunderstanding Concessions

In addition to over-conceding, making concessions that are misunderstood by the other party or not fully understanding the concessions made by the other party can damage the negotiating process. Ensuring that both parties have a clear and mutual understanding of the terms and implications of each concession is crucial for success.

Start by using clear terms in both verbal and written communication. Ambiguous language is a common source of miscommunication. Clear, specific terms are essential to ensure both parties have the same interpretation. For instance, avoid terms like *"as soon as possible."* Instead, specify exact deadlines.

Likewise, making assumptions about what the other party understands or expects from a concession can lead to misalignment. It's crucial to state expectations clearly. For example, assuming that the other party understands a discount applies only to the first order without explicitly stating it can cause disputes later.

Cultural differences in communication styles and negotiation practices can also result in misinterpretations. It is important to be aware of these differences. For instance, in some cultures, indirect communication is preferred, which might be misunderstood by parties from cultures that value directness.

Avoid using overly complex or technical language, which can obscure the meaning or value of concessions and lead to misinterpretation. Simplifying language can help ensure clarity. The language used to describe concessions should be clear, precise, and unambiguous. Avoid jargon and terminology that might be misunderstood.

Finally, confirm understanding by summarizing and restating the terms of the concession. Encourage the other party to do the same to ensure mutual clarity. Wrap up the negotiation by summarizing key points and concessions to reinforce understanding. This helps ensure that all parties are aligned.

Employing techniques to clarify and confirm understanding can avoid misunderstandings. Clear, specific language, active confirmation, and comprehensive documentation are essential for mutual understanding and preventing disputes.

Key Takeaways

Leverage and concessions are essential components of successful negotiations. Understanding and effectively using leverage can significantly strengthen your negotiating position and improve your results. Leverage comes from your unique strengths, capabilities, and alternatives, and it helps you influence the other party to agree to favorable terms.

Strategically making concessions is equally important. Concessions should be planned and executed in a way that advances your negotiation goals without compromising your core interests. They should build goodwill, foster cooperation, and move the negotiation forward. Making concessions also demonstrates flexibility and willingness to collaborate.

Mastering the use of leverage and concessions is essential for effective negotiations. By identifying and enhancing your leverage points, making well-planned concessions, and maintaining ethical standards, you can build stronger, long-term, profitable partnerships.

CHAPTER 8
Close the Deal

"Don't celebrate closing a sale, celebrate opening a relationship."

— Patricia Fripp

Do you know the most critical phase of flight for an airplane?

Takeoff and landing.

Do you know why?

These phases of flight demand precise coordination, optimal engine performance, and flawless execution of procedures by the flight crew. Any miscalculation or mechanical failure during takeoff can have catastrophic consequences. Similarly, landing requires meticulous control and judgment as the aircraft descends and makes contact with the runway. Weather conditions, runway length, and aircraft speed must be managed with utmost precision to ensure a safe landing.

In the context of closing a deal in a negotiation, the takeoff and landing phases of flight can be likened to the initiation and conclusion of the negotiation process. Closing the deal is comparable to the landing phase of the flight. It is the moment when all the efforts and negotiations come to fruition. Just as a pilot must execute a landing with accuracy and precision, as a negotiation ninja, you must finalize agreements with accuracy and precision.

Deal closure confirms that all negotiated terms are understood, agreed upon, and formally documented. Without a clear and strategic closing process, the risk of misunderstandings, unfulfilled expectations, and disputes increases significantly. Alternatively, a well-executed closing process leaves both parties feeling satisfied and confident in the agreed terms, paving the way for successful implementation and ongoing collaboration.

Closing a deal involves the following 3 key elements: knowing the right time to close, finalizing the agreement, and post-closure follow-up.

Let's take a closer look at these one by one.

Recognizing the Right Time to Close

Recognizing the right time to close a deal is a critical skill in negotiations. Fortunately, it's not all guesswork. It involves interpreting various telltale signals from the other party that indicate readiness to finalize the agreement. These signals can be verbal or nonverbal, and accurately reading them helps you close the deal at the optimal moment.

Look for Closing Signals

First, recognize that closing signals can be either verbal or non-verbal. Verbal cues may include:

Affirmative Language. Pay attention to words and phrases that suggest agreement and readiness. Positive affirmations like *"yes," "I agree," "that sounds good,"* and *"let's proceed"* are strong indicators that the other party is ready to close.

Finalizing Questions. When the other party starts asking specific questions about implementation, timelines, or next steps, it often indicates that they are thinking about how to proceed with the agreement.

Commitment Statements. Statements that reflect commitment or intent to proceed, such as *"Let's move forward," "This works for us,"* or *"We can sign today,"* are clear signals of readiness to close.

Alternatively, non-verbal cues may include the following:

Body Language. Positive body language can be a strong indicator of readiness. Look for signs like nodding, leaning forward, maintaining eye contact, and smiling. These actions suggest agreement and engagement.

Closing Gestures. Physical actions such as reaching for a pen, reviewing the contract closely, or arranging papers can signal that the other party is ready to finalize the agreement.

A Relaxed Demeanor. A shift from a tense to a more relaxed demeanor often indicates that the other party feels comfortable with the terms and is ready to close.

Of course, the clearest sign that the other party is ready to close is when they explicitly state their readiness. Phrases like *"Let's close this deal," "We are ready to sign,"* or *"When (or, How) can we finalize this?"* leave no ambiguity.

By accurately identifying and interpreting these verbal and non-verbal cues, you can recognize the right time to close the deal. Understanding these signals ensures that you finalize the agreement at the optimal moment, leading to a smooth and successful closure.

How to Gauge Their Readiness to Close

Even if the other party does not provide verbal or non-verbal cues, you can still continue the momentum of the negotiation by gauging their readiness to close. This involves assessing whether the key aspects of the negotiation have been resolved, confirming mutual readiness, and making sure that both sides are ready to finalize the agreement.

First, consult your checklist of major negotiating points. Assess whether all major points have been addressed by both parties. This may include items such as pricing, terms and conditions, delivery schedules, payment methods and dates, and any other critical issues.

Seek verbal confirmation by explicitly asking direct questions to confirm that all major points have been addressed. This helps ensure that there are no lingering concerns or unresolved issues. For example, you might ask: *"Are there any other major points we need to discuss before we finalize the agreement?"*

Additionally, summarize the agreed-upon terms and conditions at the end of each discussion. This reinforces mutual understanding and ensures all major points are covered. Ask open-ended questions to uncover any additional concerns or issues that might not have been addressed. This ensures that all potential issues are brought to light and resolved. For instance, try asking: *"Is there anything else we need to discuss or clarify before we move forward?"*

Use direct questions to confirm that both parties are ready to close. Phrases like *"Are we ready to finalize the agreement?"* or *"Can we proceed with closing the deal?"* can provide clear confirmation. Wrap up by summarizing the main agreements and asking, *"Can we proceed with signing the agreement based on these terms?"*

After confirmation, use positive statements and forward-looking language to encourage closure. Phrases like *"I'm confident this agreement will be beneficial for both of us"* can help reinforce readiness.

Finally, outline the next steps in the closing process. Providing a roadmap for finalization helps ensure both parties are prepared to proceed. For example: Explaining, *"The next step is for us to review the final contract, sign it, and then begin implementation."*

By thoroughly assessing whether all major points have been addressed and using these techniques to confirm mutual readiness, you can ensure that both parties are fully prepared to close the deal. This approach minimizes the risk of overlooking critical issues and enhances the likelihood of a smooth and successful closure.

Finalize the Deal

After the other party signals a readiness to close, it's time for the boring (or fun) part of the process to begin. This involves assembling all of the paperwork, gathering signatures, and a legal review of all of the terms agreed upon to finalize the deal.

Let's dive into this process a bit further, starting with documenting the deal.

Document the Deal

Documenting the deal is one of the final steps of the negotiation process. Both sides have worked hard to reach an agreement and have most likely made concessions along the way. The deal has evolved into something that neither party originally anticipated when they initially sat down at the negotiating table. Therefore, it is critically important to document the deal as it exists after the negotiating process is finished.

Proper documentation ensures that all terms and conditions are clearly stated, legally binding, and enforceable. This process involves preparing documentation, ensuring clarity and completeness, and obtaining formal approval from all parties involved.

The Importance of Formal Documentation

Not to belabor the point, but taking the time to get the paperwork cannot be overstated because a failure to do so can undermine all of the effort put into the negotiation.

Consider these additional benefits:

Legal Enforceability. Proper documentation creates a legally binding agreement that can be enforced in a court of law. This protects the interests of all parties involved and provides a clear reference in case of disputes.

Clarity and Precision. Proper documentation ensures that all terms and conditions are precisely defined, reducing the risk of misunderstandings and ambiguities. This clarity helps both parties understand their obligations and expectations.

Accountability. Documenting the deal holds all parties accountable for their commitments. It outlines the consequences of non-compliance, which can deter breaches and encourage adherence to the agreement.

Amendments and Updates. Formal documentation provides a structured framework for making future amendments or updates to the agreement. Any changes can be documented and signed by all parties, maintaining the integrity of the original deal.

REMEMBER: *In most cases, a contract won't be ready when the negotiation process ends because lawyers do not draft final agreements at the negotiating table. A tentative agreement is generally reached, and a Memorandum of Understanding (i.e., MOU) is signed. Then, the tentative agreement is sent off to legal counsel to finalize the terms of the contract.*

Types of Documents (Contracts, MOUs, etc.)

Very rarely is the final contract ready to be signed in an initial negotiation session. This is because several points of contention generally need to be worked out. The more likely scenario is that both parties walk away with preliminary documents and send these to their respective legal counsel to review and prepare a final contract or an addendum to an existing contract.

Here are some of the types of agreements that might be signed following the negotiation:

Memorandums of Understanding (MOUs): MOUs outline the basic terms and intentions of a deal before finalizing a formal contract. They are often used in the initial stages of negotiation to document mutual understanding.

Letters of Intent (LOIs): LOIs express the intention to enter into a formal agreement and outline the key terms. They are typically used in mergers, acquisitions, and large-scale projects.

Service Level Agreements (SLAs): SLAs are specific types of contracts that define the level of service expected from a service provider. They outline performance metrics, response times, and penalties for non-compliance.

Non-Disclosure Agreements (NDAs): NDAs protect confidential information shared between parties. They outline what information is confidential and the parties' obligations to protect it.

Purchase Orders (POs): POs are used to authorize the purchase of goods or services. They specify the items ordered, quantities, prices, and delivery details.

By preparing comprehensive documentation, you ensure that all terms and conditions are legally binding, easily understood, and enforceable. This step is essential for protecting the interests of all parties and providing a solid foundation for successful implementation.

Making Sure It's All Legal

Ensuring legal compliance is a vital step in finalizing any agreement. This involves reviewing the agreement to ensure it adheres to all relevant laws and regulations, seeking legal advice, and implementing measures to maintain compliance throughout the agreement's term. Proper legal compliance helps mitigate risks, avoid disputes, and ensure the agreement's enforceability.

Never accept a final contract written by the other party without having your own legal counsel or legal representative review and approve the agreement. There are several reasons for this, but the most important reason is that your interests need to be accurately and fairly represented and protected. This is a fact that most small business owners and entrepreneurs who negotiate with large companies miss. Take the time, spend a few extra dollars, and invest in having an attorney read and explain the contract, especially if the final terms are vague or unfamiliar to you.

A thorough legal review helps identify potential legal issues that could arise from the agreement. This proactive approach allows parties to address and resolve these issues before they become significant problems. Compliance with industry-specific regulations and standards is essential, especially in niche industries, to avoid legal penalties and ensure smooth operations.

Always hire qualified legal counsel to review any agreement (even if you write it). Legal professionals can provide expert advice on compliance, enforceability, and potential risks.

IMPORTANT NINJA TIP: Having legal counsel is especially critical if you are negotiating in a specialized space, such as cross-border trade (e.g., importing goods). Even if the agreement involves parties in different states, ensure compliance with the laws of all relevant jurisdictions, including federal laws and regulations.

Obtain Signatures

After the formal contract has been drafted and reviewed by legal counsel, it's time to "sign on the dotted line." Securing signatures is the final step in formalizing an agreement, making it legally binding and enforceable.

In the *"good old days,"* signing meant taking out a pen and physically signing your name (preferably in blue ink). Today, however, technology has made the process much easier. The recommended approach is to utilize electronic signature platforms to streamline the signing process. This method is efficient, secure, and legally recognized in many jurisdictions. For example, platforms like DocuSign or Adobe Sign allow parties to sign electronically from different locations.

IMPORTANT NINJA TIP: When obtaining signatures, make sure all parties have *"binding authority."* This means that they are considered representatives of the company, able to enter into a legally binding contract on behalf of the organization they represent.

Here are some additional points to keep in mind:

- Provide clear instructions to all parties on how and where to sign the document, including a cover letter with the contract that outlines the specific areas for signatures and initials. This helps to avoid any confusion or errors during the signing process.
- For agreements that require additional legal authentication, involve witnesses or a notary public during the signing process.
- After the signing process is complete, follow up with all parties via email confirmation to verify receipt of the signed agreement and address any final administrative details.

Employing these strategies during the signing process can ensure that all parties formally commit to the agreement, making it legally binding and enforceable. Properly securing signatures helps maintain the integrity of the agreement and provides a clear record of mutual consent.

Common Pitfalls to Avoid

When it comes to closing the deal, the biggest pitfall to avoid here is overlooking details during the final stages of negotiation. Overlooking details in the final stages of negotiation and deal closure can lead to significant issues down the line. Ensuring thoroughness and accuracy in all aspects of the agreement is crucial for preventing misunderstandings, disputes, and potential failures.

Ignoring small but important details can lead to unexpected costs and financial liabilities. These hidden costs can accumulate and significantly impact the overall profitability and feasibility of the deal.

Likewise, overlooking operational details, such as timelines, responsibilities, and resource allocations, can disrupt the smooth implementation of the agreement. This can cause delays, inefficiencies, and even project failures.

To avoid these pitfalls, be sure to involve experts, such as legal advisors, financial analysts, and industry specialists, in the review process. Their expertise can help identify and address any overlooked details.

Also, make sure that the agreement is written in clear, precise, and unambiguous language. Define all terms clearly and avoid jargon or vague expressions that could lead to misunderstandings.

Treat the agreement as a living document that may require regular review and updates. Revise the agreement to reflect these developments as new information becomes available or circumstances change.

Ensure that all parties involved in the agreement have the opportunity to review and comment on the final document. This collaborative approach helps identify any overlooked details and ensures mutual understanding.

By employing these strategies to finalize deals, you can mitigate the risks associated with overlooking small but important details. A comprehensive and meticulous approach to reviewing and finalizing agreements helps prevent misunderstandings, disputes, and operational disruptions, thereby ensuring the integrity of the deal.

Key Takeaways

In this chapter, we explored the essential steps and strategies required to close a deal effectively. Successful closing involves thorough preparation, meticulous documentation, clear communication, and proactive follow-up.

By understanding and implementing the points in this chapter, you ensure that your deals are closed successfully, delivering maximum value and fostering strong, long-term business relationships. Effective deal closure is not just about finalizing agreements but also about building trust, achieving strategic goals, and continuously improving your negotiation processes.

In our final chapter, we'll come full circle by reflecting on what went well and what lessons were learned.

CHAPTER 9
Reflect and Improve

"I do not think much of a man who is not wiser today than he was yesterday."
— Abraham Lincoln

After the ink is dry and everyone walks away from the deal, the process of negotiation comes full circle.

The ability to reflect and continuously improve is crucial for long-term success. In true ninja fashion, reflection allows you to analyze your performance, identify strengths and weaknesses, and learn from both successes and mistakes. Continuous improvement ensures that you remain adaptable, enhance your skills, and refine your strategies over time.

Reflection and continuous improvement are not one-time activities but ongoing processes that should be integrated into every negotiator's routine. This mindset fosters resilience, adaptability, and a commitment to excellence, all of which are essential for success.

Analyze Past Negotiations

Analyzing past negotiations is another essential step in the journey to continuous improvement. By examining what happened during previous negotiations, you can understand the effectiveness of your strategies and find areas for improvement. This provides a clear roadmap for future performance.

Reviewing past negotiation sessions can reveal common strategies that may not have been readily apparent at the negotiating table. For example, you might recognize common objections raised by the other party, frequent sticking points, or typical negotiation tactics used by opponents. Understanding these patterns allows you to anticipate and prepare for similar challenges in future negotiations, becoming more proactive and less reactive.

By dissecting key decision points in past negotiations, you'll gain a better understanding of what led to successful outcomes and what caused setbacks. This analysis helps hone decision-making processes.

Similarly, reviewing the tactics used in past negotiations helps determine which were effective and which were not. This helps you to refine your approach and use more suitable strategies.

Additionally, reflecting on successful negotiations helps build your confidence by reinforcing what was done well. This positive reinforcement serves as motivation to continue using strategies and techniques that yield positive results. Remember, each successful negotiation provides insights that contribute to your overall knowledge and skill set, making you more confident and capable of handling future negotiations.

You continuously refine your skills and enhance your performance by systematically analyzing past negotiations. This not only leads to better negotiation practices but also contributes significantly to personal and professional growth.

Review Key Negotiation Points

As you reflect on what went well and what could be improved, it is important to take a step back and dissect the pivotal moments that led to the final outcome of the negotiation. By identifying and scrutinizing these critical points, you'll gain insights into your decision-making process and the impact of your approach.

Let's look at each stage of the negotiation:

Preparation Stage

Setting Objectives. *How well-defined and realistic were your initial objectives?* Reflect on whether the goals you originally set were achievable and aligned with the overall strategy.

Research and Information Gathering. *How thorough was the research you conducted?* Identify any gaps in knowledge about the other party, industry (or market) trends, or competitive landscape.

Initial Discussions

First Impressions. *Did you make a positive first impression?* Consider how well your initial approach and discussions contributed to the tone of the negotiation.

Identifying Interests. Reflect on how effectively the underlying interests and needs of both parties were identified and communicated.

Negotiation Dynamics

Key Offers and Counteroffers. Review the sequence of offers and counteroffers. *Which offers and proposals were pivotal in advancing the negotiation or causing impasses?*

Emotional and Psychological Factors. *What was the impact of emotional and psychological factors on the negotiation dynamics?* Reflect on moments when emotions influenced decision-making for better or worse.

Decision Points

Critical Decisions. *Which key decisions significantly influenced the outcome?* Reflect on the rationale behind these decisions and their long-term implications.

Agreement on Terms. *How were the final terms were agreed upon? Were any last-minute changes made?* Assess the effectiveness of the closing strategies.

Decision Tree Analysis. Use decision trees to map out different decision paths taken during the negotiation. Analyze the outcomes of each path to understand the impact of various decisions.

Post-Negotiation

Implementation and Follow-Up. *What did the initial stages of implementing the final agreement look like?* Identify any challenges faced and how quickly and professionally they were addressed.

Feedback and Reflection. Reflect on feedback received from all parties post-negotiation. Consider how this feedback aligns with your own observations.

By systematically reviewing and analyzing key moments in past negotiations, you'll gain valuable insights into their decision-making processes and the effectiveness of your strategies. This reflective practice is essential for continuous improvement and achieving better results in future negotiations.

Cultivate Self-Awareness

As a ninja negotiator, you must cultivate self-awareness throughout your journey. It involves understanding your strengths, weaknesses, biases, and emotional triggers. By cultivating self-awareness, you can better manage your behavior, improve your decision-making, and build stronger relationships with your counterparts.

"Knowing yourself is the beginning of all wisdom."
— Aristotle

Tips to Increase Self-Awareness

Self-awareness does not happen by chance, nor does it exist in a vacuum. It comes from constant practice. Here are some practical tips for increasing your self-awareness:

Start by maintaining a negotiation journal to document and reflect on each negotiation experience. Write down your thoughts, feelings, actions, and outcomes after each negotiation session.

In addition to journaling, use self-assessment tools and personality tests to gain a deeper understanding of your negotiation style, strengths, and areas for growth. For example, try taking the Myers-Briggs Type Indicator (MBTI) or Thomas-Kilmann Conflict Mode Instrument (TKI)[1] to understand your natural tendencies in conflict and negotiation situations.

Work on developing your emotional intelligence (also referred to as EQ), which includes self-awareness, self-regulation, motivation, empathy, and social skills. High EQ is linked to better negotiation strategies.

Learn to handle stress by practicing stress management techniques to maintain composure and clarity during negotiations. Reducing stress enhances self-awareness and decision-making. Techniques such as deep breathing, progressive muscle relaxation, or yoga can help control stress and improve focus.

---

1. To learn more, see https://kilmanndiagnostics.com/overview-thomas-kilmann-conflict-mode-instrument-tki/

It is also important to recognize and address your own inherent biases. By acknowledging and identifying implicit biases that can affect your judgment and decision-making in negotiations, you can help mitigate their impact.

An important area of growth for many negotiators is identifying emotional triggers and acquiring strategies to manage them during negotiations. Staying calm and composed improves one's ability to negotiate effectively. Remember that aggressive negotiation tactics are often designed to trigger frustration, so practice techniques to stay calm and assertive.

Finally, remember to be adaptable. Understanding your own tendencies allows you to adapt your negotiation style to different situations and negotiating counterparts. Flexibility is key to navigating diverse negotiation scenarios. For instance, remember to adjust your approach when negotiating with a highly analytical counterpart versus a more relationship-focused counterpart.

Self-awareness helps you better understand and manage your own behavior, improve your decision-making, and build stronger relationships with your peers. This reflective practice is essential for continuous growth and success in future negotiations.

Sharpen Your Critical Thinking Skills

Critical thinking is another essential skill. It involves analyzing information objectively, evaluating different perspectives, and making reasoned decisions. This enhances your ability to assess situations accurately, identify underlying issues, and come up with effective solutions.

"No problem can be solved from the same level of consciousness that created it."

— Albert Einstein

Sadly, critical thinking is an overlooked skill in our society. We often become so enamored with what technology can do that we fail to develop critical thinking skills — reasoning that technology can do it all for us. However, as a negotiator, critical thinking will serve you well throughout your journey.

Here are some additional reasons why:

Improved Problem-Solving. Critical thinking enhances your problem-solving ability, helping you to create solutions that address the interests of all parties.

Informed Decision-Making. By evaluating evidence and considering multiple perspectives, you will make more informed and rational decisions. This reduces the risk of making impulsive or biased choices.

Improved Communication. Critical thinking improves your ability to articulate arguments clearly and logically, which enhances your communication and persuasiveness during negotiations.

Strengthened Relationships. Critical thinking contributes to a respectful and collaborative negotiation environment. You can focus on building trust and long-term relationships by understanding and addressing the other party's interests.

Increased Adaptability. By considering different scenarios and potential developments, you'll become more adaptable and better prepared to handle unexpected changes.

Fair Assessment. Critical thinking enables an objective evaluation of proposals and counteroffers, leading to fairer and more balanced agreements.

How to Enhance Critical Thinking Skills

To enhance your critical thinking skills, start by developing the habit of asking probing questions to explore underlying issues and gather more detailed information. This practice generally helps to uncover hidden interests, biases, and motivations.

Next, critically evaluate the evidence and information presented during negotiations. Assess the reliability, validity, and relevance of the data before responding or making decisions. Be sure to analyze situations from multiple perspectives to gain a comprehensive understanding. Consider the interests, constraints, and objectives of all parties involved.

Don't forget to challenge your assumptions and beliefs regularly. This practice helps identify biases and prevents them from influencing your decisions.

After each negotiation, critically analyze the outcomes. Identify what strategies worked, what didn't, and why. Use this analysis to refine your approach for future negotiations. Then, practice reflective thinking by reviewing your thought processes, decisions, and outcomes to identify areas for improvement.

Finally, don't be afraid to actively seek out and consider opinions from colleagues, mentors, and industry experts. Different viewpoints can provide new insights and challenge your thinking.

By sharpening your critical thinking skills, you can improve your ability to analyze situations, make informed decisions, and devise effective strategies. This naturally leads to better results, stronger relationships, and a greater ability to navigate more complex negotiation scenarios.

Common Pitfalls to Avoid

The biggest pitfall (or, really, obstacle) to improvement is complacency. As a negotiator, when you become complacent, you're more likely to overlook potential risks and miss opportunities for growth. The key to avoiding this is maintaining a mindset of continuous improvement.

Here are some additional reasons why complacency should be avoided:

A complacent attitude hinders personal and professional growth. When you stop honing your skills, this can result in the inability to handle new challenges. Complacency can also cause you to miss changes in the business environment, industry trends, or negotiation dynamics. Failing to adapt to these changes can put you at a significant disadvantage.

Likewise, complacency can lead to underestimating opponents and failing to adequately prepare for negotiations. This overconfidence can result in poor negotiating tactics and unfavorable agreements.

How to Avoid Complacency

To avoid complacency, set challenging and ambitious goals to push yourself beyond your comfort zone. Regularly updating your goals ensures you remain focused on growth and development.

Cultivate a growth mindset by viewing challenges as opportunities to learn and grow rather than reasons to give up. Embrace setbacks as valuable learning experiences and use them to drive improvement.

Stay informed about changes and trends in your industry. Understanding the broader context of change helps you adapt your negotiation strategies to remain relevant and effective. Then, try new strategies, techniques, and approaches. Experiment with different methods and be open to testing new ideas.

Create detailed action plans that outline the steps needed to achieve your goals. Break down larger objectives into smaller, manageable tasks to make progress more achievable. Then, prioritize actions based on their potential impact on your performance. Focus on implementing the most significant improvements first to see immediate benefits.

Also, don't forget to celebrate your achievements and milestones—no matter how seemingly insignificant. Recognizing progress reinforces a positive attitude toward continuous improvement and motivates you to keep striving for excellence.

Finally, hold yourself accountable for continuing to strive for excellence. Find a working accountability structure, such as regular check-ins with a mentor, setting deadlines, or hiring accountability partners.

By leveraging a mindset of continuous improvement, you will remain effective, adaptable, and competitive. This will support your growth and development, leading to continued success in negotiations.

Key Takeaways

By consistently evaluating your performance and seeking opportunities for growth, you can enhance your negotiation skills and achieve better outcomes. Reflection allows you to analyze your negotiation experiences, identify strengths and weaknesses, and learn from both successes and mistakes. Continuous improvement is crucial for staying competitive, adapting to changes, and enhancing your effectiveness.

Cultivating self-awareness and understanding your own biases and tendencies also enhance your negotiation performance. Developing critical thinking skills will help you analyze situations more effectively and make better decisions. Remember that continuous reflection and improvement are not just one-time activities but ongoing processes that will greatly enhance your negotiation skills over time.

Okay. There's one more thing I want to say . . .

Congratulations, Ninja!

It looks like we've come to the end of our journey together. With the information, tips, and strategies we've discussed . . .

YOU ARE A NEGOTIATION NINJA!

Thank you for the opportunity to be a part of your journey.

With Love and Gratitude,

www.ingramcontent.com/pod-product-compliance
Lightning Source LLC
LaVergne TN
LVHW090956080826
845145LV00003B/1032

* 9 7 8 1 9 6 3 2 6 7 1 1 2 *